An ABC of Early Childhood Education

This unique and engaging resource describes, critiques and analyses the significance of a wide range of contemporary and classic ideas about how young children learn. Organised in a handy A–Z format, author and early years expert Sandra Smidt

- traces back each idea to the roots of how it was first conceived;
- explores its implications for the early years classroom in accessible terms;
- makes connections where relevant to other strands in the field of early childhood education;
- provides examples from her extensive classroom experience and international literature;
- draws on a range of ideas from both developing and developed countries giving the material a truly global focus;
- uses a sociocultural view of learning to underpin the choice or analysis of each idea.

Students on early years education courses at a range of levels will find this an essential and enlightening companion text, for use throughout their studies.

Sandra Smidt is a writer and consultant in early years education. She has previously written *Introducing Freire* (2014), *The Developing Child in the 21st Century* (2013), *Introducing Malaguzzi* (2012), *Introducing Bruner* (2011), *Playing to Learn* (2010) and *Introducing Vygotsky* (2008), all published by Routledge.

An ABC of
Early Childhood Education

A guide to some of the key issues

Sandra Smidt

Routledge
Taylor & Francis Group

LONDON AND NEW YORK

KH

First published 2015
by Routledge
2 Park Square, Milton Park, Abingdon, Oxon OX14 4RN

and by Routledge
711 Third Avenue, New York, NY 10017

*Routledge is an imprint of the Taylor & Francis Group,
an informa business*

British Library Cataloguing in Publication Data
A catalogue record for this book is available from the British Library

Library of Congress Cataloging in Publication Data
Smidt, Sandra, 1943-
An ABC of early childhood education : a guide to some of the key
issues / Sandra Smidt.ISBN 978-1-138-01977-5 (hardback) -- ISBN
978-1-138-01978-2 (paperback) -- ISBN 978-1-315-77865-5
(e-book) 1. Early childhood education. 2. Early childhood education--
Research. 3. Early childhood educators. I. Title.
LB1139.23.S64 2014
372.21--dc23
2014010060

ISBN: 978-1-138-01977-5 (hbk)
ISBN: 978-1-138-01978-2 (pbk)
ISBN: 978-1-315-77865-5 (ebk)

Typeset in Optima
by Saxon Graphics Ltd., Derby

Printed and bound in the United States of America by Publishers Graphics,
LLC on sustainably sourced paper.

5/9/16

This book is dedicated to the many children who have enchanted, engaged, outraged and surprised me over many years with their comments, creations, ideas and invention and to the many adults whose ideas have helped me come to understand just how vital it is to nourish curiosity, questioning, creativity, collaboration and relationships. As Vivian Gussin Paley tells us in her book *Bad Guys Don't Have Birthdays*:

> Watching him with the five-year-olds, I saw, finally, how the method worked. He'd ask a question or make a casual observation, then repeat each comment and hang on to it until a link could be established to a previous statement. He and the children were constructing paper chains of ideas, factual and magical, and Bill supplied the glue.
>
> But something was going on more important than method: Bill was truly curious. He had a few prior expectations of what kindergartners might think or say, and he listened with the anticipation we bring to the theater. He was not interested in what he knew to be the answer; he wanted to know how the children approached the problem.
>
> (Paley, 1988, pp. 7–8)

Bill was a teacher of older children who had asked Paley if he might spend some time with the kindergarten children in order to come to understand the continuum of learning and growth and the impact (potential and actual) of schooling. This book is for all the Bills and Paleys and the bad guys who don't have birthdays.

Preface

This is not the sort of book you read from cover to cover. Rather it is a book to dip into when you want to find information or refresh your memory. It is a list of some of the key ideas or concepts in early childhood education, organised in alphabetical order with the key concepts elaborated and some less significant sub-concepts defined.

Guide to using this book

Arranged in alphabetical order are a number of *key concepts*, themes or issues in the world of early childhood education. They are all set out in almost the same way and one issue can lead you to another. They are accompanied by concepts that are less important, which I am calling *sub-concepts*, and these are merely defined, together with details of which key concepts they relate to.

Underneath the title of each key concept are words that are *synonymous with* it, just in case you know it by another name. So, for example, 'active learner' is synonymous with 'meaning-maker'. Some of the synonyms are close rather than identical in meaning. And for some I could find no synonym.

This is often but not always followed by a *table of words or phrases linked with the concept, what they mean and why they matter*. In the text that follows any word defined and analysed in the table will usually be found in italics. Other words in italics may not be included in the table because their meaning will be apparent to you but they are words to become familiar with.

After that is the *body text* telling you about the concept, and embedded in this you will usually, but not always, find *examples* or *case studies* together with *samples of the writing style of some of the authors and researchers in the field*. These are here to allow you to consider whether you might like to read more of their work. There is then a section on the *implications of what you have read for your practice*, a list of the *other key concepts related to the one you are reading* and an *annotated further reading list*.

This may be a reference to a whole book, a chapter in a book or an article in a journal. Some of the references offer you a link so that you can read the article online.

This book does not have any of the following:

- A glossary, since all new terms are defined and explained within the text;
- An index, since finding your way around the book is very straightforward. Each of the key concepts and sub-concepts tells you where to find related issues in the text.

I have had great fun designing and writing this book and hope you have fun using it.

Abstract:

A thought or idea that does not have a concrete or physical presence.

See also key concepts: Attention, bilingualism, cognitive development, first-hand learning, interaction with others, intersubjectivity, play, roles

Active learner, the child as

Synonymous with: The child as meaning-maker, child constructing meaning

Words or phrases linked to this concept	What it means	Why it matters
Interactions with others	Being part of groups of people or living in a social world	Much is written about the importance of children learning with and from others
Communicating with others	From birth children are communicating with others using sounds, gesture, expressions and language(s)	Communication is vital to successful learning and teaching
Assimilation	Take in new information	For Piaget both of these are fundamental to learning
Accommodation	Change what is known in response to something new	
Construct or make meaning	From before birth the human infant explores everything in order to make sense of the world	The human infant should always be seen as being active and not passive

Piaget was remarkable in the sense that he was the first to describe the child as an active learner, a constructor of meaning. Until Piaget wrote about this the human infant had been seen as passive, waiting to be taught everything that she needed to learn. Through his careful and detailed observations of his own children he was able to illustrate how, from birth, young children use all their senses and movement of parts of their body to make sense of this world they inhabit. We are used to this but it was quite revolutionary at its time and certainly made all those involved in the lives of young children reconsider how to both work and interact with them. Seeing babies as competent, and young children as problem posers and problem solvers, is something we find in all good early years practice.

Vygotsky viewed babies and young children as active learners. For him, the learning took place not only through their explorations of objects in their world but also, and importantly, through their *interactions with others*. So babies and young children are constantly trying to make sense of the sounds they hear (particularly the words of the languages of their homes) and other aspects of life that define them as human. They are involved, from the start, in *communicating with others*. They are also participating in the rules and rituals, practices and beliefs, customs and values specific to their cultures.

Piaget and Vygotsky both arrived at the realisation that from birth children *construct or make meaning*, and based their findings on what they had studied and read as well as on their own observations of children in different settings and situations. Piaget, as you might know, was working in Switzerland, while Vygotsky lived, studied and wrote in Russia. Vygotsky's work translated into English was published at more or less the same time as Piaget's work and both exerted a profound influence on psychologists, writers, thinkers, linguists and others. To see the child as working to understand the world from the moment of birth was a truly revolutionary concept.

Case study/example

> When Hannah was 12 weeks old her grandmother recorded in her developmental diary that she had, by accident, kicked the bell attached to an elephant mobile over her cot. She then repeated this action again and again, sometimes smiling at the bell and sometimes crying in frustration.

It is tempting to think about this in fairly simple terms. By accident the child's foot touched the bell, which then rang. The child liked the sound of the bell ringing and kept repeating an action to achieve a desired goal – the bell ringing.

Does that offer an adequate explanation of the child actively seeking to make sense of the world? Piaget might have analysed it in terms of *assimilation* (taking in new information and adding it to what is already known) and *accommodation* (having to change thinking in response to something new that has been experienced), which he regarded as the building blocks of cognition. For Vygotsky something is missing from that analysis. In order for the child to realise that she has caused the bell to ring, the child has to have a sense of her own agency – her ability to make things happen in her immediate environment.

In his own words

Vygotsky wrote in Russian, which is translated into English, and you may struggle to make sense of some of his work as it can be quite dense and academic.

> It is through the mediation of others, through the mediation of the adult, that the child undertakes activities. Absolutely everything in the behaviour of the child is merged and rooted in social relations. Thus, the child's relations with reality are from the start social relations, so that the newborn baby could be said to be in the highest degree a social being.
>
> (Vygotsky, 1997, vol. 4, p. 281)

 ## *Implications for early years practice*

All those involved with the learning and development of young children do accept how hard they work to make sense of every aspect of their lives. For Piaget the young child was a tireless little explorer and scientist; for Bruner and Vygotsky the child's meaning-making extended to the social, cultural and emotional worlds. Where Piaget believed that the role of the teacher was primarily to set up a challenging and enriched environment, Bruner and Vygotsky placed more emphasis on the role of the teacher and peers in learning, on communication and language(s) and on the essential significance and contribution of culture and context.

 See also: Cognitive development, collaboration, decentre, expert others, language acquisition, meaning

 ## *Annotated further reading:*

Halfpenny, A. and Pettersen, J. (2014). *Introducing Piaget: A guide for practitioners and students in early years education*. London and New York: Routledge.

Smidt, S. (2009). *Introducing Vygotsky: A guide for practitioners and students in early years education*. London and New York: Routledge.

Smidt, S. (2011). *Introducing Bruner: A guide for practitioners and students in early years education*. London and New York: Routledge.

These three books are all in the series called 'Introducing…' published by Routledge. They are guides to some of the most prominent theorists and purposely written in an accessible but unpatronising tone.

Agency

Synonymous with: Ownership, being in control or in charge, able to see the purpose

Words or phrases linked to this concept	What it means	Why it matters
Sociocultural approach	An approach that always sees that the context and the culture need to be considered, not just the individual	Living in a world with others is always the context for any analysis of people
Dialogic approach	Where the learner is not seen as an empty vessel but as an active participant	Teacher and learner become equal partners in a situation where both can ask and answer questions
Cultural capital	What you know	What you know comes from who you are, where you live and what experiences you have

Since children are continuously making sense of their world they need to develop the sense of agency – their own ability to contribute to, participate in or take control of something. Bruner (1996) said that agentive mind is 'proactive, problem-orientated, attentionally focused, selective, constructional and directed to ends' (p. 93). We can say that agency, or the ability to actively participate, is the realised potential – what we actually do – of people to act on their world purposefully in interactions where different courses of action are possible and desirable, depending on the participant's point of view. You will appreciate that using the term 'agency' implies a *sociocultural approach to learning* – seeing it always set in the context of a culture and a society. Bruner moves on to saying that someone with an agentive mind is not only active, as we have seen, but also works out dialogue and discourse with others with other active minds. This is how we come to know others – what they think and feel and believe.

Case study/example

Bruner offers the example of Ann Brown, in the Oakland Project, who developed a classroom culture that required both agency and collaboration. The children were encouraged to ask questions, develop theories, talk to others about them and make changes. In this setting each child is both learner and teacher. It is what Paulo Freire would have called a truly *dialogic approach*.

Agency is closely related to two other important concepts: identity and power. If you think about yourself you can see you that your identity might seem different according to where you are and who you are with. The same is true of children.

The child who is a newcomer to a class may well feel totally powerless and become silent and unable to integrate, despite being a live wire in other contexts. A girl in a space dominated by boys might equally lose all sense of her own self-worth. Children who are deprived of a voice become silent and more passive: those whose agency is thwarted become alienated.

Pierre Bourdieu was a sociologist who carefully examined power and class. One of his interests was why certain groups in society succeeded while others did not. One of the concepts he developed was that of *cultural capital*. This refers to what people know and it will not take long for you to realise that what you know depends largely on where you live, with whom and in what circumstances. In a way this analysis suggests that we are passively dependent on our circumstances but Prout (2005) argued that children, as active agents, can not only acquire more capital but can appropriate and transform capital.

In her own words

Priscilla Anderson talks of how infants and young children develop a sense of their own agency from birth.

> Babies take part in a 'cultural life and the arts' when they are first wrapped or clothed, hear a lullaby and their family language and smell food cooking. Breastfeeding depends on the baby's expressed 'views' about setting the pace and timing and the 'demand' that builds up the supply. By proxy babies enjoy their parents' rights to freedom of association and peaceful assembly, to information, thought, conscience and religion, and they suffer if these rights are denied through family poverty or persecution. Young children soon learn when they are cold enough to need a coat, and tend to assert their autonomy and dignity through strenuous resistance to being strapped into a pushchair without warning or negotiation.
>
> (Anderson, 2010, in Percy-Smith and Thomas, pp. 90–91)

Implications for early years practice

All of you involved with young children will be aware of how they continue to construct and transform their images of themselves as they build their self-concept or identity. Some will have to struggle with issues such as gender identity where the ideas of the home are different from those of the classroom or with speaking languages other than English when that is not encouraged. All will have to construct an image in the new context of the setting or classroom. In order for them to be able to do so successfully they need to be supported in following their own interests and passions rather than being required to do too formal activities too early. In other words they need to have time to make their own choices, decide for themselves what they want to do and how. Only in doing this – i.e. playing – can they be agentive.

 See also: Bilingualism, culture, interaction, intersubjectivity

Annotated further reading:

Percy-Smith, B. and Thomas, N. (2010). *A handbook of children and young people's participation: Perspectives from theory and practice*. London and New York: Routledge.

A collection of writings about children's rights in many countries. Although the focus is not really on young children, many of the issues discussed are relevant and there is much that is interesting and informative in this book.

Apprentice, child as

Synonymous with: Active participants, guided participation

Words or phrases linked to this concept	What it means	Why it matters
Cultural tools	These are the objects and signs and systems that we, as human beings, have developed over time within our own communities to help communication and thinking	We all come from cultures that have developed their own cultural tools. All learners need access to cultural tools to help them make sense of the world
Mediated by	Something that facilitates or helps learning and moves between the learner and the thing to be learned	Mediation was key to Vygotsky's thinking and is firmly rooted in his view, which was social and cultural
More expert other	Vygotsky was clear that not only adults could take learning further. Children who have more experience or more knowledge of a task can support the learning of a less experienced learner	A reminder that children learn through all their encounters and that children can teach and learn from one another
Active participants	Play an active role in learning	They are both learner and teacher
Guided participation	Children learning alongside more expert others usually in real-life contexts	Children learn through all their encounters and experiences
Make human sense	Where the purpose or the point of something is clear to the learner	Reminds us of the significance of children not being asked to do meaningless tasks

The term 'apprentice' is often used to describe young adults placed alongside competent others, learning from them. Vygotsky, in his sociocultural analysis of learning, saw that young children learn from everything and everyone and much of this learning is *mediated* through the *cultural tools* of any society. Here we encounter some tricky vocabulary so we will spend some time defining what we mean.

This is all quite complex when you first read it but once you think of it in everyday terms you will see just how much sense it makes. To help you do this try to work out what is happening in each of these small examples.

Case study/example

Try to identify the learner (in this case the less expert other), the *more expert other* and the cultural tool, if there is one.

Sacha's dad is reading him a Russian story from a picture book. When his mum is there she sings him English songs.

Xoliswe carries her baby sister on her back talking to her all the time as she points things out.

Quite simple, really. Sacha is the less expert other in the first example and his father the more expert other. Sacha is learning about his father's culture and language (Russian) from the cultural tool of a book. When his mother is there she uses the cultural tool of song to mediate Sacha's understanding of her language and culture. So in each case Sacha's experience of the world is being mediated by a more expert other.

Xoliswe, who is only nine years old, is the more expert other. She knows more and has had more experience than the baby on her back. The baby's experience of the world is being mediated by Xoliswe using the cultural tool of spoken language and pointing out objects. The significant thing here is that more expert others can be children.

Vygotsky did not use the word 'apprentice' but you can see how the learners are effectively apprenticed to those who have more knowledge or experience. This idea of mediation was taken on by the American researcher Barbara Rogoff. She worked not only in the United States but also with communities in developing countries where she noted how children are more involved in the real life of families and community than they are in much of the developed world. This meant that they were *active participants* in the processes, routines and rituals of adult daily life. She watched as children were inducted into the particular practices of families and communities through what she called *guided participation*. This guided participation was sometimes through being alongside an experienced person watching what they were doing, sometimes through social interaction such as talking about what was being done and sometimes through direct teaching. Her view of development involved three interacting planes on which development occurs. These are: the individual plane within the child herself; the social plane, involving other people within the community within which the child lives; and the actual sociocultural context that defines the manner in which these people engage in the processes of making and sharing meaning.

Can you see how this view allows her to analyse the learning she sees taking place in terms of the time and place, the culture and the context?

> Three children are alongside their mother who is making tortillas on the fire. She gives them each a lump of dough and they watch what she is doing and imitate her, throwing the dough, flattening it and rolling it. They watch not only their mother but also one another. Here they are doing and memorising individually as they are involved with other people within the cultural context of making the bread of their community.
>
> (Adapted from the work of Rogoff)

In her own words

> Development is a process of people's changing participation in the sociocultural activities of their communities.
>
> (Rogoff, 2003, p. 52)

As you can see, she writes in an accessible style and voice. What would you say is important about what she says here? My understanding is that what is important is that we cannot see development itself as a universal term. Rather, it must involve the acquisition of those skills and knowledge practices that are important to the community involved rather than to a generalised community. Making tortillas requires similar but not identical skills to making bagels, pita bread or focaccia, for example.

Implications for early years practice

Rogoff's work in general is a reminder of the importance of taking account of the context in which the children are learning. She reminds us that children learn wherever they are and do so alongside and from their peers as well as adults. By looking at the children in their homes and communities she is inevitably looking at learning situations that make *human sense* to the children. They can see the purpose of the activities. This is a reminder to us to offer such opportunities for young children whenever we can.

She also reminds us that children learn not only at school or in a setting, but everywhere and the learning that takes place away from our eyes and ears must be valued and respected. She spoke of children being apprentice learners throughout their lives.

 See also: Guided participation

 Annotated further reading:

Rogoff, B. (1990). *Apprenticeship in thinking: Cognitive development in social context.* Oxford: Oxford University Press.

Rogoff, B. (2003). *The cultural nature of development.* Oxford: Oxford University Press.

Rogoff, B., Mistry, J., Goncu, A. and Mosier, C. (1993). Guided participation in cultural activities by toddlers and caregivers, *Monogram of Social Research, Child Development, 58*(8), Serial no. 236.

Rogoff refers to many real-life examples and does not use too much academic jargon. I find her work easy to read and she certainly adopts a broadly sociocultural approach, which I like.

Arts:

The expression of ideas, thoughts and feelings through painting, sculpture, making, music, writing, drawing, dance, song, etc.
See also key concepts: Agency, creativity, culture, representation

Asking questions

Synonymous with: Developing theories, hypothesising, posing questions, raising questions

Words or phrases linked to this concept	What it means	Why it matters
Schematic behaviour	Repeated patterns of behaviour like sorting, transporting, enveloping	Reveals what questions children might be asking themselves
Higher order functions	Where the learner is conscious of what she is doing	Drawing on memory enables the learner to do more and more complex things
Cognitive development	The development of thought	Thought governs all our behaviour
Ongoing collaborative story-making	A way of teaching where children make stories about what interests or concerns them	One of the prime ways we make sense of our lives is through narrative
Pedagogy of listening	The art of teaching based on listening	Only in this way can adults know what children are interested in and can do
Theories	Children develop their own ideas about the world and what is in it	Listen out for them!
Culture of listening	Where it is clear that the voice of everyone is important	Builds respect for others
Metaxis	The ability to think about 'what if?'	A significant higher order skill
Pretend/fantasy play	Where children create and inhabit possible worlds	Using the imagination plus memory plus much more

It took a long while for theorists and psychologists to accept the constructivist view of children as active learners and a longer time for them to consider seriously the fact that children constantly ask questions using words when they are able, but also through their actions. Here is an example of a very young child exploring the world.

Case study/example

> Harry draws lots of circles and spirals. He chooses round shapes when making models. He spins round in the playgroup. He holds a long ribbon in one hand and moves it in a circular pattern in the air.
>
> (Smidt, 2013a, p. 123)

Is this haphazard and random behaviour? Is Harry mucking about or bored or being silly? Perhaps he is asking himself some questions about things he has noticed in his environment. Perhaps he is asking himself if something round will always be round. Will it still be round on the ground as well as in the air? Will it still be round if it is moved? If he makes a big movement will he be able to make a big circle? If he makes a small movement will he make a small circle? These are merely my suggestions. Only Harry knows what questions he is raising. This is an example of *schematic behaviour* where the child engages in repeated patterns of action – a behaviour that often seems inexplicable to adults but is, in fact, just part of the active exploration of the world. You may have come across children who transport things from one place to another, or who like to cover things up or who suck or grasp everything. As they do this they are almost certainly engaged in trying to find the answers to some question in their minds.

Piaget was interested in the child, as explorer, finding things out and answering questions through exploration. But he was little interested in linking this to the questions children raise as they explore or try to make sense of events or objects. Vygotsky, with his interest in the vital role played by language in learning, was aware of the importance of the questions children raise as they explore, play and interact. He saw questioning as one of what he called the *higher order functions* in *cognitive development*. The first well documented evidence of an interest in children's questions was the work of Susan Isaacs at the Maltings School, which culminated in her book, *Intellectual Growth in Young Children* (1930, first edition). It is full of serious, funny, brilliant and original ideas raised by the children, all illustrating how many questions children ask and try to answer. Later, Vivian Gussin Paley, a kindergarten teacher in the United States, included the entire kindergarten curriculum in every aspect of the classroom where she spent her time listening to the children, hearing their spoken questions, and understanding those not spoken but apparent from what the children were doing. In the now famous nursery schools developed by Loris Malaguzzi in Reggio Emilia, a *pedagogy of listening* was put in place. What the educators were doing was listening to and looking out for the questions the children ask in order to arrive at the *theories they develop*. Theresa Grainger, working with slightly older children, developed a classroom *culture of listening*. This is where children aged between seven and nine use drama as a tool for creating *metaxis*, which is a set of higher order functions that allow the learner to hold the ideas of the actual, the possible and the 'what if'. This has clear links to what children do in their *pretend or fantasy play*.

In their own words

Susan Isaacs kept detailed records of what the children said and did. Here is part of an enormous list of some of the everyday facts they questioned:

The cooking of toast, cocoa, fruit, vegetables. The boiling of water – the small bubbles of air and the larger bubbles of steam; the rate of burning of different substances such as wool and cotton, held in the Bunsen flame; dissolving of sugar in warm water. The rate of melting snow and ice and different conditions and the amount of water produced; the making of ice, and the fact that a small quantity of shallow water froze more quickly than a larger amount.

(Isaacs, 1930, p. 285)

Gussin Paley's style is more narrative. Here is her account of what happened when Lisa brought a picture of her new baby sister to the class.

Rose:	Does she have a name?
Lisa:	Nancy Lynn.
Wally:	Is she white?
Lisa:	I think so. I didn't see her yet. She's still in the hospital.
Deana:	She has to be white because Lisa's whole family is white.

(Paley, 1981, p. 162)

At the end of a discussion Deana dictated a complicated story all about a little girl who had to take care of the baby and the adventures the mother had going into the forest to get some food. There was a hunter and a tiger, footprints to follow and much more.

Rinaldi's voice is somewhere in between and we need to remember that we are reading it in translation. Here is what she says about the purpose of questioning for very young children. What she is asking is: why do children ask questions?

From a very young age, children seek to produce interpretive theories, to give answers. Some may say these theories are ingenuous and naive, but this is of little importance: the important thing is not only to give value to, but above all, to understand what lies behind these questions and theories, and what lies behind them is something truly extraordinary. There is the intention to produce questions and search for answers, which is one of the most extraordinary aspects of creativity.

(Rinaldi, 2006, pp. 112–113)

Implications for early years practice

It is really worthwhile stopping your normal practice in order to spend more time just watching and listening to the children. You need to do this with respect and attention and ideally you need to take some notes. Because what you are looking for is what it is the child or children are paying attention to. What are they interested in? What is raising questions in their minds? Only by doing this can you successfully support their learning.

 See also: Active learner, cognitive development, complex environments, culture of listening, document, emotional development, formats, play, relationships, scaffolding

 ## *Annotated further reading:*

Isaacs, S. (1930; 1938). *Intellectual growth in young children*. London: George Routledge & Sons Ltd (out of print).

Paley, V. G. (1981). *Wally's stories: Conversations in the kindergarten*. Cambridge, MA and London, UK: Harvard University Press.

Rinaldi, C. (2006). *In dialogue with Reggio Emilia: Listening, researching and learning*. London and New York: Routledge.

Smidt, S. (2013a). *Introducing Malaguzzi: A guide for practitioners and students in early years education*. London and New York: Routledge.

The Susan Isaacs book is out of print and that is a shame because it is just wonderful, as are all of Vivian Gussin Paley's books. She was a kindergarden teacher and a wonderful teller of tales. Her books are a treat!

The Rinaldi book is fairly straightforward to read. It contains many fine things and is useful if you are particularly interested in Reggio Emilia.

Attention

Synonymous with: Concentration, diligence, engrossment, immersion, thinking

Words or phrases linked to this concept	What it means	Why it matters
Attention	Take notice of something	One of the higher order skills showing the ability to concentrate
Higher order function	Being consciously able to do something. For example to make intentional movements, concentrate, or organise things into categories	For Vygotsky the fact that they are conscious is the vital thing. Lower mental processes are more closely related to feelings and biological needs
Memory	An everyday word whose meaning you will know	It is through memory that learners internalise experiences and become aware or conscious of what they know
Signs	A sign is something that stands for or represents an object or an idea. A triangular sign in the UK represents danger	Part of the system of semiotics (see below)
Semiotics	The study of symbols or signs	Much of what children learn at school involves the use of signs and symbols
Formats	One of Bruner's key terms meaning the ways in which adults support and scaffold the learning of young children	Comes about through repeated actions and games involving anticipation played by parents/ carers with children

Attention is an everyday term, which is used in many situations and contexts. In early childhood education it is often used pejoratively to describe a child who does not conform to the social rules and expectations of the setting. I am sure you have encountered children who are said to have a limited attention span and perhaps even children who are said to suffer from Attention Deficit Hyperactivity Disorder. For Vygotsky *attention*, together with *memory*, is a *higher order function* and is mediated by the use of *signs*.

Those interested in infants often base their research on how attentive they are to changes in the environment. Colwyn Trevarthen (1977), for example, showed that infants aged only 2 months respond differently to someone in the room who speaks to them from someone who remains silent. Johnson (1990) showed that newborn infants pay closer attention to an object with a face-like array on it than to the same shape with an abstract array of marks. So attention – looking closely at something, listening intently to sounds – is a key indicator of the beginning of thought.

We now come to the issue of shared attention or intersubjectivity, much studied and discussed over the last few decades. It means just what is sounds like – the sharing of attention involving two or more participants in an event. Bruner wrote a great deal about this and was initially prompted by a paper presented by Daniel Stern in 1982 who had examined what happened when the mother began to introduce an object into her interactions with the baby, which became a clear target for sharing attention. Bruner was very interested in what happened during such exchanges and noticed that when mother and baby were focused on the same thing eye contact become more sustained and the mother tended to talk more to the baby about the object. Then the baby joined in vocalising. Mother and baby began to take turns. So this is social, interactive, and the beginning of *formats*. This was one of the key terms in Bruner's work and describes the ways in which adults in particular are able to scaffold the learning of children through repeated actions or routines. Later the baby and mother will use eye-pointing and pointing in order to share attention.

So the attention of the babies is an indicator of the beginnings of higher order mental functioning and also a tool for those researching child development. As children get older attention also indicates their involvement in what they are doing. Sensitive practitioners use this to assess not only the child but their own practice. In settings where the interests and concerns of the children are paid attention to by the staff, children are almost always deeply involved in what they are doing. So when people tell me that young children have a limited attention span I know that the fault does not lie within the child.

Case study/example

I love these diary entries made by Charles Darwin as he observed his newborn first child.

My first child was born on December 27th, 1839, and I at once commenced to make notes on the first dawn of the various expressions which he exhibited, for I felt convinced, even at this early period, that the most complex and fine shades of expression must all have had a gradual and natural origin.

(Darwin, 1887/1958, p. 131)

During the first seven days various reflex actions, namely sneezing, hiccuping, yawning, stretching, and of course sucking and screaming, were well performed by my infant. On the seventh day, I touched the naked sole of his foot with a bit of paper, and he jerked it away, curling at the same time his toes, like a much older child when tickled. The perfection of these reflex

> movements shows that the extreme imperfection of the voluntary ones is not due to the state of the muscles or of the coordinating centres, but to that of the seat of the will.
>
> (Darwin, 1877, p. 285)

> Darwin was just one of many who kept diaries of his children's development. Many of those who did note just how intently children begin to pay attention to others, even in the presence of new and interesting objects. Babies look at other babies; they try to pull hair and touch noses; they exchange wary looks and smiles. Their world is a social one.

In his own words

Colwyn Trevarthen writes with simplicity and humour and his work is a pleasure to read:

> Most impressively, an alert newborn can draw a sympathetic adult into synchronized negotiations of arbitrary action, which can develop in coming weeks and months into a mastery of the rituals and symbols of a germinal culture, long before any words are learned. In short, a human being is born capable of seeking and playing with others' attentions and feelings in a rich variety of provocative, humorous and teasing ways (Reddy, 2008). Infants, it appears, are born with motives and emotions for actions that sustain human intersubjectivity. They perform actions that are adapted to motivate, and invest emotions in, an imaginative cultural learning (Trevarthen, 2001a; Bråten and Trevarthen, 2007). Their intelligence is prepared to grow and be educated by sharing the meaning of intentions and feelings with other humans by means of many expressive forms of body movement that may be perceived in several modalities.
>
> (Trevarthen, 2010, p. 3)

Implications for early years practice

Do not believe that anyone in your group has a limited attention span. Rather try to find out what all the children, as individuals, are interested in and fascinated by. Then build your curriculum around these interests. If you pay attention to the children you can set up a curriculum that will meet both individual and group needs. And hand control to the children; allow them to be agents largely in charge of their own learning. This means allowing them to play and to use all the languages available to them – verbal, symbolic, artistic, musical, dramatic, narrative, investigative – to raise and answer questions.

See also: Creativity, DAP, document, emotional development, formats, guided participation, identity, interaction, intersubjectivity, language, mark-making, monologues, narrative, relationships, representation and re-representation, role, rules, scaffolding

📖 *Annotated further reading:*

Trevarthen, C. (2010). What is it like to be a person who knows nothing? Defining the active intersubjective mind of a newborn human being. *Infant and Child Development,* Special Issue, Edited by Emese Nagy. Available at:
www.psych.uw.edu.pl/lasc/Trevarthen2.pdf.

This is the first suggested reading of a journal article and it is written in fairly academic language, but try reading Trevarthen's work. It is always interesting and you should manage to understand most of it. To read it just enter the link into your web browser.

Becoming a reader

Synonymous with: Able to lift the tune from the page

Word or phrase linked to this concept	What it means	How we use it
Phonemes	A distinct unit of sound	Allows us to distinguish one word from another – e.g. bat vs. hat
Consonant blends	Two or three consonant sounds that can each be heard when pronounced	In the word 'drink', for example, you can hear the 'd' and the 'r' sounds

Learning to read in literate societies happens when children are in the early years and despite volumes having been written on the subject it is still a contentious issue in this country. We start with how Henrietta Dombey explains what makes learning to read different from learning to write, despite having features in common.

In her own words

Henrietta Dombey says:

> Children learn to talk through being involved in conversation, being given turns, listened to and responded to. They don't learn by being taught all the phonemes of spoken English, one at a time, with no real involvement in communication until they know all 44. Instead the most successful learners are engaged in complex interactions from a very early stage, encouraged and supported in the business of building meaning through language.
>
> Of course we can take this parallel too far. Learning written language is not like learning spoken language. There's not the same pressing communicative need and

it doesn't happen as easily for most children. Very few children fail to learn to talk. Our brains may be wired for us all to learn to talk, but they are certainly not wired for us to learn to read: we have to do some very deliberate learning, laying down a mass of new pathways between very different parts of the brain if we are to learn to read fluently (Wolf 2008).

What this means is that we need to recognise that there are two sides to learning to read: the technical business of 'decoding' or identifying written words, and the business of using those words to communicate and think with. The same is true for writing. Of course, in both cases, there is an interaction between the technical and the meaningful aspects.

(Dombey, 2010, pp. 120–121)

That makes perfect sense to me and I hope it does to you too. Let us now look at some of the things we know. We know that English is not a phonetic language. Young children learning to read Italian do so with relative ease because words are simply structured, end in vowels and the 25 *phonemes* of the language are represented by 24 letters of the alphabet and eight two-letter combinations. The Italians have what is called a shallow orthography, which means the relationship between the phonemes and the letters is usually consistent. Lucky Italian children – although it is interesting to note how many fewer children's books are written in Italian than in English. By contrast, our wonderful language is made up of words that are full of *consonant blends* (like strength) and we do not have a consistent spelling system. This was brilliantly illustrated by George Bernard Shaw who offered up the word (or non-word in today's parlance) 'ghoti' for readers to decode by using phonics. Can you do this? The word is 'fish' and this is how you can sound it out: gh = f as in rough, o = i as in women and ti = sh as in nation. English children are bound to have more of a struggle to decode words in isolation, dependent on rules that are so often broken. They do need to learn the sounds of letters individually and in combination but the question is when and how.

We know too that children who have had a lot of experience of being read to are more likely to learn to read with ease. Dombey tells us that some children starting in early years settings will have had experience of over a thousand story-readings in English with parents or carers. Some will come with similar experience in other languages. Some will have had little or no experience at all.

We know that children today see print all around them and certainly on mobile phones, computers, television screens and tablets. They are accustomed to living in what we might call a digitally literate world.

We know, perhaps most importantly, that those children who encounter models of readers in their lives and are drawn into the wonders of narrative through words and pictures develop a love of reading. Reading for them is making meaning – lifting the tune from the page. And if we want our children to become truly literate we have to help them know that reading is about meaning. Being able to decode isolated words or non-words out of context has nothing to do with making sense of the world.

I now want to introduce you to a wonderful little book written by Margaret Meek and called *How Texts Teach What Readers Learn*. In this book of only 48 pages she makes clear how the makers of children's picture and story books induct children into different worlds and at the same time into the conventions of storytelling and literacy. You would do better to spend most of your time with young children in telling and reading stories than getting them to recognise the sounds made by letters. Here is what Meek tells us:

> We learned to read competently and sensitively because we gave ourselves what Sartre called 'private lessons', by becoming involved in what we read. We also found we could share what we read with other people, our friends, our colleagues, our opponents, even, when we argued with them. The reading lessons weren't part of a course of reading, except of the course we gave ourselves in our interaction with texts. If we can at this point acknowledge the importance of those untaught lessons, I think we should look at them more closely, beginning with the beginners.
>
> (Meek, 1988, pp. 6–7)

Try to highlight the key words for you in that passage. I highlighted 'becoming involved'; 'share'; 'interaction with texts' and 'untaught lessons'.

Case study/example

If you want to read an excellent account of one child becoming a self-taught reader you should read Bissex's GNYS AT WRK, which you can find referenced under 'Mark-making'. Here is a small extract from it to give you the sense of what she is saying as she writes about her own son, Paul.

> A month later, with *Ape in a Cape*, which had been read aloud to him and which provided rhyme and picture clues for some words, Paul read 'pig with a wig', 'rat with a bat', 'whale in a gale' – though after deciphering 'gale' correctly, he wondered if it was right because the word was unfamiliar to him. … Books were not Paul's basic reading materials, however, until he developed more fluency. …When he had a book he tended to focus on the captions. For instance in Richard Scarry's *What Do People Do All Day?*, a favourite book, he enjoyed reading little signs amid the illustrations, such as 'mail', 'baggage', 'hospital'
>
> (Bissex, 1980, p. 123)

Implications for early years practice

Read the work of people like Frank Smith, Henrietta Dombey and Margaret Meek to get a sense of the ongoing debate about how best to teach reading. If you want to persuade people of your ideas you need to be well informed. Set up your provision so that there are many opportunities for all types of literacy and communication. In the home corner have opportunities for reading and remember signs and labels and instructions can all be read. Build up a library of excellent wordless books, picture books, songs and rhymes, story books. Take advice. Read to the children as often as you can and invite them to share books with one another, with other adults and with you. Make reading a high profile but not a testing activity. Sharing books should be intensely pleasurable.

 See also: Cognitive development, language, mark-making, meaning, rules

 ## *Annotated further reading:*

Meek, M. (1988, first published). *How texts teach what readers learn*. Stroud: Thimble Press. An amazing little book, which is, hopefully, still in print.

Dombey, H. (2010). It all starts with /c/a/t/ – or does it? Foundation phonics. In S. Smidt (Ed.), *Key issues in early years education*. London and New York: Routledge.

Becoming a writer:

How children come to make sense of the written word and generate rules that they try out, evaluate, and transform
See also key concepts: Becoming a reader, cognitive development, decentre, expert others, guided participation, mark-making, rules

Bilingualism/multilingualism

Synonymous with: Speaking two or more languages

Words or phrases linked to this concept	What it means	Why it matters
Metalinguistic	Knowledge about language itself	Helps in learning additional languages
Everyday concepts	The language of normal daily life	The only way in which young children can communicate
Scientific concepts	The language of exploration and analysis	The more complex language required for abstract thinking
Creative thinking	The ability to come up with new ideas or views	To be creative is to be able to think differently or create new things
Sensitivity to communication	The ability to recognise different languages	A higher order skill that most bilinguals have

We live in a world where people move from country to country in search of work, freedom or a better life and it is apparent that most developed countries now have large numbers of people living in them who speak two or more languages. In our schools and settings we will find very young children and their parents who do not yet speak English or who speak a little English plus the languages they speak at home. The children will learn English almost by default. They will learn it because it is the language of the television and the internet and of the school or setting. They will learn it most effectively if they are encouraged to use it in conjunction with the languages they have already acquired.

Schools and settings throughout Europe and North America have experienced linguistic and cultural diversity for many years and it is surprising and disappointing that controversy about this still rages. Yet the evidence from years and years of research is clear and important: denying people access to their home language(s) means not respecting their languages, cultures and identities. It sets up a two-tier society within the school or setting with the 'good' people speaking English and the others not. Instead of seeing difference as something to be celebrated it is seen as 'the problem'.

Jim Cummins has spent his academic life arguing that mother tongue should be used, supported, respected and even taught in schools. Working in Toronto he has considered the issue carefully and in a paper published in 2001 and available freely online he cites some of these research findings. They are summarised here:

- If young children are allowed to develop their first languages throughout the primary school years they understand more about language itself and how to use it effectively. Knowing about language is called metalinguistics. When children develop literacy in more than one language they are able to compare and contrast how the two languages organise and reflect reality.

- Children who come to school with a solid foundation in their mother tongue develop stronger literacy abilities in the host language. When parents and grandparents and carers are able to spend time with children reading or telling stories, singing songs, cooking or playing in the first language children develop a wider vocabulary and set of skills and concepts in the home language. They are developing what Vygotsky called everyday concepts, which are precisely those they will need in order to acquire the more abstract scientific concepts. All this helps them be ready to tackle a new language and new set of concepts and skills.
- Maintaining mother tongue helps children develop not only mother tongue but also cognitive skills, which help children perform well in school in all the traditional mainstream subjects.
- Spending teaching time on using more than one language does not hurt the academic development of anybody. Mother tongue speakers feel accepted and valued. Monolingual children learn something about how other languages work. The Foyer project in Belgium develops children's spoken and literacy abilities in three language (whichever is their mother tongue, Dutch and French) throughout the primary school and is proving to offer one of the best examples of the benefits of bilingual or trilingual education.
- Mother tongue use is fragile and easily lost. With its loss there is a loss of identity and culture and the risk of the loss of strong familial links. So rejecting a child's language is tantamount to rejecting the child.

Colin Baker, in a report he gave to the Welsh Assembly, highlighted the cognitive gains offered by being bilingual. He examined a body of research covering over 20 years. Here are his findings:

1. Having two well-developed languages can give people particular advantages in thinking, rather than making them mentally confused, as is sometimes alleged. These advantages apply to four areas, as follow:
   i. *Creative thinking*: bilingual children have two or more words for each object and each idea. When different meanings are attached to words in the two languages, a bilingual person must develop the ability to think more flexibly.
   ii. *Sensitivity to communication*: bilingual people have to know which language to speak with whom, and when. Monolinguals often need to select a style of discourse and a tone of voice and sometimes even a special vocabulary according to the audience. We speak differently to our parents from the way in which we speak to our friends; differently in the classroom from in the playground. Bilingual people tend to be more sensitive to the needs of listeners than monolingual people.
   iii. *Tests and scores*: for what it is worth, bilingual people do better on IQ tests compared with monolingual people of the same socioeconomic class.

iv. *A head start in reading*: bilinguals being less fixed on the sound and more centred on the meaning of words have been shown by Canadian researchers to have a head start in learning to read. Think about the implications of this in light of our insistence on adopting a phonic- rather than meaning-based approach to learning to read.

2. Being able to switch naturally between languages, and being able to talk to different people in those languages, makes children feel good about themselves and their abilities. A sense of real ownership of both languages and cultures can do wonders to help raise a child's self-esteem.

(Baker, Rapporteur Group on Bilingualism to Welsh Assembly.
Available at: www.assemblywales.org/paper_3_-_prof._colin_baker.pdf)

Case study/example

Maureen Turner (1997) describes what happened to Rameen who came to England at the age of four, at a time when she was still making sense of her world using her first language of Urdu.

In her first year at school she did well, learning to speak English, beginning to read and write in English, adapting to a new environment and culture, overcoming some confusion during maths lessons and establishing a very strong bond with her teacher who was keen to ensure two things – one was that Rameen did well at school and the other that Rameen did not lose her Urdu and hence her links to her parents, grandparents and culture. To ensure this the class teacher involved Rameen's mother in the life of the school. This partnership minimised the difficulties for Rameen and built strong links between school and community.

In the classroom a hospital area was established and became a popular centre for role play. Rameen chose to play in there, being familiar with hospitals since her aunt was at the time in one. Here is a transcript of the play that followed and the language used by the children involved. Notice how fluent Rameen is in the context of play in a situation familiar to her.

Rameen: I know what the police number is – 999. The doctor is asking someone if they're a patient and someone comes in.
Linda: Let's put it over there …
Rameen: I'm putting some clothes on this one (baby doll).
(She finds a 'please be seated' notice).
I can put this on the table. This can be the waiting room.

In their own words

Turner, an experienced and highly regarded teacher of bilingual children, says this:

> From our joint observations of Rameen and the background information from her mother, we felt that she had come into English before she had fully sorted out early concepts in her mother tongue. There has been much interest in recent years about the effect of the age of entry into a second language. Cummins (1984) argues strongly that second-language learning will be more effective if a child's mother tongue is well-developed. When the first language is less secure, and when a child is immersed in a second language every day at school with a corresponding lack of incentive to develop home language, the learning of, and in, the second language may be impaired.
>
> (Turner in Gregory, 2004, p. 139)

Implications for early years practice

Ignore those who tell you that children must use English at all times if they are to succeed at school. There is evidence from across the world that children who are able to keep their first languages maintain their sense of identity, remain able to be in touch with close family members and enjoy cognitive advantages in terms of linguistic facility, communicative sensitivity and metalinguistic skills.

Reflect the languages and cultures of the children in your group and never tell parents not to use their first languages with their children.

 See also: Culture, egocentric, feelings, identity, language acquisition

Annotated further reading:

Gregory, E. (Ed.) (2004). *One child, many worlds: Early learning in multicultural communities*. London: David Fulton Publishers.

Gregory, E., Long, S. and Volk, D. (Eds) (2004). *Many pathways to literacy: Young children learning with siblings, grandparents, peers and communities*. London and New York: RoutledgeFalmer.

Eve Gregory is the editor of both these books, which means that she has collected together works by different authors around a particular topic. You will see that her interest lies in culture and literacy. Her books are a delight and you can pick and choose from many different authors, voices, opinions and chapters.

Cognitive/intellectual development

Synonymous with: Cognition, thinking, problem solving

Words or phrases linked to this concept	What it means	Why it matters
Age-related stages	That children learn differently according to their ages	Largely discounted although evident in our school system
Schemas	Repeated patterns of behaviour	Help to interpret children's behaviour in terms of learning
Adaptation	Piaget's word for learning, and meaning the ability to adjust to new information and experiences	Explains how we adapt to changes
Equilibration	Another of Piaget's terms and one difficult to explain	Piaget believed this allowed children to move from one stage to another
Intermental	Means it happens between people	Vygotsky talked of this in terms of language acquisition
Intramental	Takes place within the learner	Vygotksy talking again of language acquisition that moves from intermental to intramental
Internalisation	One of Vygotsky's key terms meaning something that goes in and takes place in the mind or head and is not evident	When this happens the child is able to deal with ideas and concepts without having to have the object or event at hand
Enactive stage	Bruner's first stage of representation where the child uses movement and the senses	The beginning of being able to use tools to represent ideas and feelings
Iconic stage	The second stage of representation using images and pictures	The use of a wider range of cultural tools
Symbolic stage	The third stage using symbols	The last and most abstract stage

This is an enormous area of study because those of us involved in the education and care of young children place huge emphasis on how successfully we manage to help children reach particular milestones or targets in their learning. In many places this takes precedence over all other aspects of development – sometimes at some cost to the individual child. We will start again by looking briefly at what Piaget thought about cognition. You may know that he believed that children proceed in their thinking through *clear stages and these stages are age-related*. Each stage is characterised by different types of thinking, which he referred to as mental structures or operations. In short he believed that the thinking of a toddler was different from that of a school child, which was different from that of an adolescent. This view has been much disputed. Piaget also observed that young children often engage in repeated patterns of behaviour that look random but are in fact serious. They are attempts to classify and categorise as the child makes sense of the environment and the objects in it. He called these *schemas* and they are prevalent during infancy. They later become elaborated and internalised – although this was not a term Piaget would have used. A central theme in Piaget's thinking was that of *adaptation*, which was the term he used for making sense of the world. Adaptation comes about through the two processes of assimilation, where children take new information into their existing schemas, and accommodation, where children change or adapt their schemas to fit new information. He talked, too, of *equilibration*, which implies a balance between assimilation and accommodation, which he believed children arrive at much later as their thinking becomes more complex. That is very much a perspective on his view of cognition in a nutshell.

For Vygotsky cognition was more gradual and nuanced and, of course, social. All learning takes place in a context. The child's understanding of the world and the objects, events and people in it is mediated by more expert others and through the use of cultural tools. Concepts or thoughts are not fixed but change and develop over time. Vygotsky talked of everyday concepts – the ideas children develop through their everyday lives around things such as eating and cooking, birth and death, sickness and health, going on holiday, staying at home, working in the fields or on the street corners. These are the spontaneous concepts that children come to understand through everyday life. He also talked of scientific concepts, which are the sorts of things children learn more formally and usually at school. These are primarily to do with more abstract concepts such as long and short or dark and light. For Vygotsky spoken language was the cultural tool through which most learning is mediated. He said that in the early stages this is *intermental*, which means that it takes place between people involved in the same activity and then becomes *intramental*, which means that it takes place within the child and this happens through *internalisation*.

Memory plays a huge part in cognitive development and it is memory that allows knowledge to be internalised. The internalisation of knowledge allows for the learner to be conscious of what is known and to be able to reflect and consider.

Three additional factors relate to cognitive development and these are imitation, questioning and elaboration. Children often start off by copying or imitation. They then internalise what they have done and this perhaps raises a question in their minds and allows them to elaborate or transform what they have done or thought.

For Bruner there was also a suggestion of cognitive development moving through stages although these were not age related. First there was an enactive stage where the child is thinking whilst manipulating objects. Is this learning through play? The second stage is the iconic stage where the child is able to make a mental image of something and no longer needs the physical object to be present. Here memory clearly comes into play. The final stage is the symbolic stage where the child is able to use abstract ideas to represent the world. The child uses signs and symbols to allow her to think critically.

Case study/example

Shirley Brice Heath (1983) tracked what a small child called Vilgot did in coming to understand what a book is and what it is used for. His initial actions and interactions depended to a large extent on imitation.

- At the age of 14 months he came across a book in his collection of toys, opened it, turned the pages and made sounds that were very like talk. In doing this he demonstrated an awareness of how adults sometimes make speech sounds as they turn pages.
- At 22 months he responded to an adult's suggestion that they should read a book and chose a large novel. The adult sat with him on the floor, turned the pages and made up a story. The child listened, looked at the pages every so often and was quite satisfied with the whole event. Here his actions indicated that he knew that a book carried a story which he could listen to.
- Four months later he picked one of his own books and handed it to his grandmother. She could not read without her glasses so she started telling the story from memory. Vilgot stopped her and instructed her to read it properly. At that point he knew that there is an invariant pattern to the book. So he was aware of the text itself, what it was and what purpose it served, although he did not yet know the word 'text'.
- At 30 months he chose a book for an older child and brought it to an adult who offered to read it to him. He turned the pages back and forth and then declined the offer, saying 'No, there is too much text in this book'. An extraordinary moment indicating that he had understood what the word text meant and made a judgement that too much text meant that the book might be boring for him.
- Just before his third birthday he asked the adult to write all the names of his family members and some other words using alphabet blocks. Whilst

the adult was doing this he picked out and pointed to the letters of his own name, saying 'It's in my name' every time the adult used that letter. His awareness now included a recognition of individual letters.

Children focus their intention on what interests them. That is why play – the ability to explore in depth the things that interest the child – is so important. When a child displays an interest in something it is likely that their existing knowledge or understanding about an aspect of the object or situation has been challenged and thus raised some questions in the mind of the child. What do you think Vilgot in the example above might have been interested in? What questions did his interactions around books raise in his mind? Perhaps he asked what the black marks on the page were for. Maybe he wanted to know what they were called. Or perhaps he asked why there were spaces between groups of black marks. *Learning is the way in which children move from what is still unknown by using what is known.* Each example of Vilgot's interaction with books shows him building on what he has learned in order to answer a question he has set himself about what he still does not understand. He shows us that learning requires the ability to transfer a skill or a memory for use in a different situation or context.

(Smidt, 2013b, pp. 122–123)

This is a long and sometimes complex extract but it does illustrate just how one child gave evidence of cognitive development.

In their own words

For Loris Malaguzzi (1993) the co-construction of knowledge is an essential ingredient in cognitive development. Here is what he says:

Children learn by interacting with their environment and actively transforming their relationships with the world of adult things, events and, in original ways, their peers. In a sense children participate in constructing their identity and the identity of others. Interaction among children is a fundamental experience during the first years of life. Interaction is a need, a desire, a vital necessity that each child carries within. … Children's self-learning and co-learning (construction of knowledge by self and co-construction of knowledge with others), supported by interactive experiences constructed with the help of adults, determine the selection and organisation of processes and strategies that are part of and coherent with the overall goals of early childhood education. … Constructive conflicts (arising from the exchange of different actions, expectations and ideas) transform the individual's cognitive experience and promote learning and development. Placing children in small groups facilitates this process because among children are not strong relationships of authority or dependence; therefore, such conflicts are more attractive and advantageous. … If we accept that every problem produces cognitive conflicts, then we believe that cognitive conflicts initiate a process of co-construction and cooperation.

(Malaguzzi, 1993, pp. 11–12)

Remember that this has been translated from the Italian and remember, too, that Malaguzzi, like all of us, is reflecting on a particular culture and context. Despite that, he offers much food for thought.

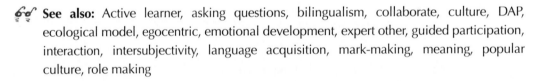 Implications for early years practice

We need to be aware of children's prior experience, respectful of other cultures and languages, attentive to children's need to have time to be alone and to be with peers in small groups. We need to think about all the children as competent and curious seekers of meaning and set up activities as best matched to the observed interests of the children as possible. We need to avoid formal teaching and to think about some of the following issues, addressed in this section. These include recognising:

- the significance of repeated patterns of behaviour;
- the social and interactive nature of all learning;
- that children learn from adults and from peers;
- that memory and language are highly significant in learning;
- that children need to experience everyday concepts through purposeful activities before moving on to more abstract events;
- that children who are able to follow their own interests become deeply engaged.

See also: Active learner, asking questions, bilingualism, collaborate, culture, DAP, ecological model, egocentric, emotional development, expert other, guided participation, interaction, intersubjectivity, language acquisition, mark-making, meaning, popular culture, role making

Annotated further reading:

Malaguzzi, L. (1993). For an education based on relationships. *Young Children*, 11(93), 11–12.

Smidt, S. (2013b). *The developing child in the 21st century: A global perspective on child development*. London and New York: Routledge.

This is my book on child development where I try to reflect aspects of child development not set in a solely Western or developed-world perspective.

Collaborate/collaboration/collaborative/co-constructor

Synonymous with: Doing/playing/working together; joint action, sharing decisions/
activities/perspectives, intersubjectivity, shared learning

You may notice that the headings of this table are different from that of other tables and
might like to think about why this is so.

Words or phrases linked to this concept	What it means	What skills are required
Agreeing	Through discussion coming to accept one view or argument over others	The ability to listen, to decentre and to change one's mind
Choosing	Selecting to do, reflect on, try, make or choose something	The ability to evaluate in order to make a choice out of possible alternatives
Communicating	The ongoing process of sharing ideas and involving listening, questioning, answering and more	The ability and willingness to listen respectfully to the views of others and offer one's own
Deciding	Rather like choosing, this is making a choice after having reflected on it or discussed it	Rather like choosing but more final, this involves the ability to discriminate carefully between options, ranking them
Evaluating	Being able to critique something and doing this without hurting someone's feelings	Judge what someone else has done and have some sensitivity to the feelings of others
Negotiating	The tricky art of putting forward a a point of view but being willing to listen to the points of view of others and through discussion or persuasion coming to a shared conclusion	Social and personal skills of listening, taking account of the views of others while trying to argue for what you have chosen
Participating	Joining in as an equal partner in an exchange of ideas or actions with others	Enough self-esteem to join in with others and offer ideas, help do things and be a partner in the enterprise
Questioning	The way in which something of interest to a learner can be developed through the raising of questions	The skill of thinking about something and finding what aspects of it are interesting, challenging and make you want to go further
Reflecting	Thinking about and evaluating what has been done	Looking at what has been done and thinking about what worked and what did not, what needs changing or elaborating
Transforming	Changing what has been made or done or decided	The ability to reflect and on the basis of this make changes to what has been done or made. Highly creative.

The layout for this concept is slightly different from that of others because understanding is most likely to come through analysing the case studies of collaborative learning that I could find – all drawn from Reggio Emilia with its philosophy of offering a pedagogy of relationships, of questioning and of listening. Several concepts are grouped together here, all with the shared meaning of learners learning alongside others, peers or adults, in joint action to make meaning. Although we do see children doing things alone, most of their activities are social and involve aspects of communicating, negotiating, choosing, agreeing and deciding. These are what Vygotsky might have called scientific concepts or processes and demonstrate higher order thinking skills.

To an effective collaborator, able to participate as an equal in any exploration, the child must be able to follow the steps required to work effectively with others. The table above is made up of some of the skills shown by children when playing or collaborating with others and these are arranged alphabetically rather than suggesting a sequence of events. As you will see, the table offers you some words relating to thinking, defined together with the particular skills a learner must have acquired in order to perform these. For example, in order to get someone to agree with you, you must be able to communicate your idea, listen to the response and perhaps change your point of view.

Now read the case study below and take Luigi and his friends and the teacher as those to study. Make your own list for both the learners and the teacher:

Case study/example

Four-year-old Luigi says to one of the adults that the birds outside the window looked bored. When the teacher responds by asking why he thinks they are bored he says that they don't have anything to do. The teacher listens carefully, takes notes and begins to think about where to take this. Luigi has expressed a concern about something he has noticed. The adult interprets this as the child empathising with the birds and internally both raising and answering questions about why this might be so. She decides to take this further, thinking that there is potential in this for much learning – and not only for Luigi.

In an English nursery class the teacher might bring in books with pictures of birds or stories about birds. She might set up a bird table. The children might be asked to draw birds.

In Reggio what happened was that Luigi was invited to tell some of his friends about what he was thinking. The other children were interested and a lively discussion took place with the teacher sitting by, taking notes, sometimes contributing, always ready to respond to what was said. The children decided that what the birds needed were things to play on – the sort of things they found in the parks and gardens and squares of Reggio. They decided they would plan and build playground equipment for birds.

They visited a local playground, taking their drawing materials with them so that they could draw the equipment there. On their return they went out into the garden to choose a possible site for their bird playground. They began to design and draw the things they would make – swings, slides, a roundabout, a climbing frame, a bench to perch on. They then discussed and asked the teacher to make a list of what materials they might need. The list included wood, glue, string, wire, empty cartons, paper clips and more. In the days that followed the children, using their drawings as plans, set about making the playground equipment. There was much discussion about how the things they were making could be made to move, whether they would be strong enough to hold the birds, how many birds could use each piece, how they would be made to stand firmly on the ground. A great deal of problem solving, measurement, estimation, exploration of balance and weight, rotation and movement, as you can see.

When the playground was ready one child asked if the teacher thought that the birds liked the playground and this led to another part of the project, where the children began to keep watch on the bird playground, taking turns to count (using a simple system of tallying) the number of birds using each piece of equipment to see which was the most popular.

(Smidt, 2013a, pp. 36–38)

I propose analysing this in terms of what the child did and what the teacher or adult did in response, charting the whole chain of events. Look out for the child as active learner and the adult as co-collaborator. Look out too for signs of higher order thinking skills.

- The child expressed an idea: the teacher listened attentively. The child *communicated* and the teacher listened.
- A dialogue between two *participants* followed.
- The adult *suggested* the child *share* his ideas with friends. The adult *observed* and *recorded* what happened.
- The adult *arranged* for the children to visit a children's playground and *organised* drawing materials to take on the visit.
- The adult set up possible *resources* for the children to use in their design and planning.
- The adult *recorded* what the children said they needed for the next stage.
- Children talked, offered ideas, raised questions, listened to one another, shared, planned and supported one another.

- The children worked alone or collaboratively *making and evaluating* their items. The teacher was on hand to *interact, support, and record*.
- Another child *expressed a related interest* and the planning and doing cycle started again.
- Now remind yourself that the children in this example were aged only four and be astounded at their higher order thinking skills.

In her own words

It is the sociocultural theorists who have written most about collaboration and learning. Certainly Vygotsky did, as did Michael Cole. For Barbara Rogoff, learning with others is essential to being human. Where children work together to make decisions they seem able to overcome initial differences to arrive at an acceptable conclusion. Rogoff cites several examples to support her arguments.

> The collaborative process seems to lead to a level of understanding unavailable in solitary endeavour or non-collaborative interaction … Miller (1987) claims that this collective process in children's argumentation with adults and peers functions as a basic developmental mechanism. He gives the example of five-year-olds arguing about the behaviour of a balance scale, with one child centering on weight as the principle for explaining what will balance, and the other focusing on distance from the fulcrum as the crucial factor. In insisting on their own perspectives, the children clarify the problem to themselves and to each other in their co-construction of the argument. If the children get to this point in argumentation, they arrive at two equally justified standpoints that exclude each other. The principle of consistency requires them to change the collectively valid to resolve the contradictions.
>
> (Rogoff, 1990, pp. 178–179)

Implications for early years practice

Setting up a classroom or setting to support collaborative learning means moving away from considering Piaget's lone scientist and considering groups of children who can choose to do things together in order to share what they know and can do with others. For those in settings with younger children this is easier to do because fewer constraints are imposed on educators from above. Nonetheless it is important to try to consider doing this wherever you are working. The focus has to shift not only from the individual to the group but from competitive learning to shared learning. We often group children by ability because it seems to make the task of teaching simpler. In reality, however, where children can choose whom to work with and what to work on (and you will realise that work here means, primarily, play) they can be both teachers and learners, supporting and learning from one another. They have more chance to develop the list of higher order cognitive skills listed in the table above.

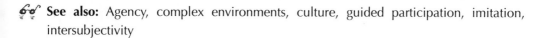 **See also:** Agency, complex environments, culture, guided participation, imitation, intersubjectivity

📖 *Annotated further reading:*

Rogoff, B. (1990). *Apprenticeship in thinking: Cognitive development in social context.* New York and Oxford. Oxford University Press.
Another interesting book from Rogoff, which is worth reading.

Smidt, S. (2013a). *Introducing Malaguzzi: A guide for practitioners and students in early years education.* London and New York: Routledge.

Common sense thinking:

The thinking we use in our everyday lives
See also key concepts: Cognitive development, first-hand experience

Competent babies:

All human babies are born with the capacity to start and continue to make and share meaning
See also key concepts: Cognitive development, emotional development, language acquisition, neuroscience

Complex or enriched environments

Synonymous with: Well-resourced

Piaget, you will remember, talked of the teacher as being responsible for structuring a rich environment in which she could take note of what the children were doing and thinking. Interacting with others was seen as being 'off-task' and was to be discouraged. In this rich environment there would be things to explore, tools to support exploration and adults on hand to keep things organised. And in the Reggio Emilia pre-schools an enormous amount of time and money is spent on setting up the most amazing places of learning anyone can imagine. Each has its own atelier, or studio, together with an artist and an enormous number of resources for drawing, painting, making and more.

This all sounds fine. We all enjoy being in places that are well laid out and where there are interesting things to do and see. But – and it is a big but – the implication is that if children are in a less richly resourced setting they will learn less. What do you think of this? Do you believe it to be true? Now read the quotation below and see if your mind is changed.

Case study/example

'Enriched environments' enhance the brain's capacity for learning.

This myth states the idea that children should be exposed to rich and diverse stimuli, i.e. an 'enriched' environment during the time they are most receptive to learning (assumed to be the time from birth up to three years of age). As a consequence, the common belief is that if a child has not been fully exposed to an enriched environment, it will not 'recuperate' later on in life and has lost capacities early in life. This would mean that for full learning to occur, rich diversity and early exposure are important.

The idea that the most effective educational interventions need to be timed with periods during which children are most receptive to learning may have arisen from influential work on early learning in rats. This research showed that rats, which were reared in an enriched and stimulating environment, exhibited a better capability to solve and learn complex maze problems compared to rats that were raised in a deprived environment. Looking into the brain of these rodents, researchers found that neurons in rats, which were raised in an enriched environment, had formed more connections, i.e. synapses and expressed more proteins associated with the maintenance of synaptic contacts (Falkenberg et al. 1992). Thus it seems, that experience tunes the wiring diagram between neurons of the brain (see Greenough, Black & Wallace, 1987). However, further research is necessary to be able to transfer these insights from animal research to human learning. As well it should not be forgotten, that the human brain shows plasticity throughout the whole life and is not limited to an 'enriched' environment phase during the first three years of life.

(Goswami, 2004, p. 11)

Goswami reminds us to be very wary of applying research with rats to children. She reminds us that recent neuroscience finds no evidence for critical or sensitive periods for learning and that human beings continue to learn throughout our lives. Those are the scientific findings and I totally accept them. But there are other concerns and for me these are more significant.

If children need enriched environments in order to learn what happens to the majority of the world's children who live and learn in poverty with limited access to early years education and almost certainly no access to the riches to be found in some provision in the developed world? Does this mean that children in developing countries will learn less than their more fortunate peers in other places? I am certainly not saying that resources and facilities do not matter. They do, but we need to remember that since children are born curious and actively make meaning from all their experiences, they will learn whether they have a home corner, a sand table, a water tray, a garden area, mirrors set into the floor or on the ceiling, or not.

Case study/example

Radhika Viruru has written a great deal about the effect of colonialism on many in the developing world. Her emphasis is on how negative this has been in many countries across the world. She spent time looking at nursery education in South India (2001) and found that they had made a conscious and political decision not to spend money on fancy resources but to rely on children's curiosity and imagination. The concept of play as the prime way of learning in the developed world seemed to them dependent on resourcing. They used the local environment plus things like lengths of fabric, found objects and the items of everyday life.

In her own words

As my work in Hyderabad, India has shown, educators there, even though they engage with children in work that is thought-provoking, and designed to meet the needs of children within that culture, both feel and are told that the work they do is inappropriate, since it does not conform to Western (mostly play-based) methods. My ethnographic work in India (Viruru, 2001) gives details about such methods of education. Although when I began this ethnographic work, I did not consider the study as operating through a postcolonial framework, the concerns that emerged from it led to its adoption. My work discusses how Western notions of childhood resemble Western notions of the Orient: based only partially on fact, but mostly on a fiction created through a combination of desire and the needs of the marketplace. This study also comments on the discourses of materialism that have invaded early childhood education, where the doctrine of children learning by doing, is interpreted more and more as justifying the need for material things in classrooms. Such an obsession with materials not only creates a larger market but also denies children the opportunity to create meaningful and self-directed social relationships among themselves.

(Viruru, 2005)

For me this is a very persuasive and important argument.

Implications for early years practice

Do remember in all your planning that you are catering for the needs of individual children who will learn from others but draw on their previous experiences, which may well be very different from one another. Try as best you can to ensure that all children will find something familiar to them to make them feel part of the group and to allow them to make human sense of the activities on offer. Encourage collaboration and sharing and show respects for all aspects of diversity – language, experience, gender. Build a culture of listening, questioning, relationships and respect.

See also: Active learner, asking questions, ecological model, neuroscience

 ## *Annotated further reading:*

Penn, H. (2005). *Unequal childhoods: Young children's lives in poor countries*. London and New York: Routledge.

Helen Penn and I were colleagues some years ago. She has travelled widely to consider early childhood in different countries and cultures and she takes a strong political stance in all of her work. Do try to read some of it.

Concepts:

Thoughts, ideas
See also key concepts: Agency, bilingualism, cognitive development, collaboration, first-hand experience

Cooperative play:

Play with another child in a negotiating manner
See also key concepts: play

Creativity/child as creative thinker

Synonymous with: Originality; consider and make something new by analysing, imagining, inventing, transforming, adapting, combining; willing to accept change and novelty; play with materials found, natural, made, everyday as well as cultural tools; divergent thinking

Words or phrases linked to this concept	What it means	Why it matters
Novel or unorthodox solution	Something never done before	This is a sign of the learner being able to invent
Competent at birth	This really means that the human infant is born ready to make sense of the world	Reminds us not to underestimate the capacities of babies
Divergent thinking	Bringing things together in new and inventive ways	Helps us encourage children to explore and try things out
Possible worlds	This is not the real world but other worlds we might invent or imagine	Young children try out roles and other things in their attempts to make sense of the real world
Atelier	Means a studio	All the pre-school settings in Reggio Emilia have studios well equipped and often with an artist in residence
Prior experience	Everything that has already been experienced	Essential for building up knowledge and understanding of the real world and beyond
Imitation	It means copying but is very significant, as you will see later in this book	One of the main ways in which children and others learn
Represent and re-represent	To draw or write about or express in other ways ideas, thoughts and feelings and then do this again	Trying out different ways of saying or expressing something is important in development
Hundred languages	Malaguzzi's term for all the expressive languages	Writing drawing, composing, playing, inventing, etc.
Symbolic representation	Making one thing stand for another	Essential for learning and development

Creativity is a word that is used in many different contexts and to describe a host of activities or ways of doing. For our purposes we are going to think about creativity as being able to consider the world and the things and people in it from different perspectives to arrive at a *novel or unorthodox solution*. A writer of fiction, for example, creates or makes up a narrative in which invented people's lives, experiences, feelings and actions are explored. A successful novel is one that throws some new light on reality. A composer uses the sounds made by instruments and combines these to create something completely symbolic but that nonetheless has the power to touch and move listeners.

But now let us look at what creativity involving young children might look like. Here we will examine a series of examples. In each one see if you can decide two things: first what makes what the child or children are doing creative, and second what the practitioners have done to encourage children to be creative.

Case study/example

The first case study comes from Reggio Emilia where the children at the Diana pre-school were designing a new curtain for the theatre.

> The painting is almost finished when Leonardo asks 'Why don't we put in some cells that come from outer space. And then they can decide what shape they want to be.'
>
> There followed a prolonged discussion about what a cell looks like and one child suggested looking in a book, another said he did not want to do that because he had a picture of cells in his mind. At this point a little girl called Mimi got up and started moving around in a spontaneous dance whilst the others drew their ideas of cells.
>
> (Based on Smidt, 2013a, p. 89)

The second example is drawn from the work of Gunther Kress whose particular interest here was in how very young children use whatever is at hand and turn it into something else:

> … a six-year-old child and her friend made a car out of two wire-mesh drawers used for storage, a pillow, a red toolbox and an assortment of other bits and bobs, passengers included. The toolbox serves as a bonnet, the two flanking drawers are the car doors, the central pillow is/are the car's seats on which – for a while anyway – the two six-year-olds were happy to sit.
>
> (Kress, 1997, p. 31)

The finished product has all the things that these children decided are essential to cars – seats to sit on, doors to get into it and a small bonnet at the front. You may be intrigued by the fact that wheels do not feature in what is essential for them.

The third example comes from Reggio Emilia again.

> Federica, aged three years and two months wanted to show a running horse in her drawing. She knew that horses have four legs and her solution to the problem she had set herself was to draw a figure of a horse with two legs on one side of the piece of paper and then turn the piece of paper over to draw two legs alone on the other side. She managed to find a solution – her own unique solution – to a problem she has set herself.
>
> (Based on Rinaldi, 2006, p. 15)

Would you agree that all the children cited here are being creative? Federica is certainly doing something new. It is almost impossible that she will ever have seen a horse represented with two legs on one side of the paper and two on the other. But what a brilliant and logical solution she has arrived at. She is truly a creative thinker.

Rinaldi has written about creativity as a quality of thought. Think about that for a moment before reading on. How does Federica's horse suggest something about the quality of what her thinking? For Rinaldi the human infant is *competent* at birth, constantly trying to make sense of, understand and interpret the world and the people and objects and events in it. In the search for meaning, the child implicitly or rarely explicitly asks questions and sets out to try to find answers. In doing this the child begins to generate theories. Leonardo's theory is that cells have minds of their own so are in control of their own destiny. The two little car makers have a theory that anything you can sit in and pretend to drive is a car. And Federica has a theory that if a horse has two legs on each side of its body the only way to show that is to show two on each side of a piece of paper. These theories may be very simple or very sophisticated. They may be nearly correct or wildly wrong. But they illustrate how hard each child is working to make sense of the world. Competent children, indeed!

Rinaldi says that the kind of thinking children display when they are being creative is *divergent thinking*, which means that they bring together things that do not normally go together and they are able to do this because they do not yet have a theoretical framework to determine what is correct. If you intend to make a car to serve your own purposes whatever you say is a car is a car. You do not have to know that some essential things required for a car are an engine, a steering wheel, wheels and brakes in order to make one that suits your purpose.

Bruner talks of the actual world and *possible worlds*. Possible worlds are those that are created in the imagination and by children largely through role play and fantasy play. Here they create worlds with their own laws and rules, customs and conventions, which can be changed at will.

When children are offered multiple opportunities to *represent and re-represent* what they see, think about, dream about, are scared of they begin to understand how many languages – expressive languages – they have at hand. They can draw and paint and make models; they can make up music, invent rhythms, create words and strings of words; they can tell and explain and describe and question; they can guess and try to evaluate and try again; they can move and dance, climb and jump. They can use any or all of the *hundred languages* Malaguzzi talked about provided they are in a setting where there is a culture of doing this. Very young children do this and to begin with they use *imitation* by copying those with whom they interact and using what is to hand. You will all have seen children putting a wooden block to their ear to be a mobile phone; pretending a ball is a spaceship; turning a toilet roll holder into a telescope. They are engaged in *symbolic representation* where one thing stands for or represents another.

In his own words

Gunther Kress wrote his book *Before Writing: Rethinking the Paths to Literacy* in 1997 – nearly 20 years ago. At that time, like now, there were things happening in our society that raised many fears in the minds of educators and carers, as the divide between rich and poor widened and life, for many, was worsening. The last paragraph in this book is what I want to quote here because it is a cry for starting up the debate about what future we want for our children and grandchildren.

> My own aim is simple enough. I would like a future for my children in which they can lead productive lives, in a society which is positively engaged with the challenges of its time, and in which despair is, at the least, balanced by hope, difficulty by pleasure. I happen to believe that the possibilities of communication are an essential foundation for that. As I am working in an environment in which it is my responsibility to think about that, in general, and in the specific terms of curricula, it is, as I see it, my responsibility to do the kinds of rethinking that I am engaged in, and to put my ideas into the public domain for examination and debate. I think that the meaning-making practices of the young humans which I have observed are a very good starting point for that rethinking, and for such a debate.
>
> (Kress, 1997, p. 164)

 ## Implications for early years practice

I wonder what you have thought about what it is that practitioners have to do to build a culture of creativity in the classroom or setting. This will be more fully discussed in the section on documenting children's progress because one of the most important things that practitioners have to do is pay close attention to what children say and do. In other words practitioners have to watch, listen, take notes, read the notes, think about them, do something in response and then start the process all over again. They also need to know as much as possible about each child's *prior experience* and about each child's lived lives. In other words they need to know about each child's *culture*.

Of course the practitioner will want to consider how to set up the environment to encourage children to use all their expressive languages. We are not fortunate enough here to be able to afford an *atelier* and an artist in every setting, nor can we ensure that there will be funding for expensive art and craft materials. But do remember that children will learn and create wherever they are and with whatever is at hand. So the focus of your planning for creativity should be on what you will do and not on what you will provide.

See also: Asking questions, culture, decentre, interaction with others, meaning, mark-making, representation

📖 *Annotated further reading:*

Kress, G. (1997). *Before writing: Rethinking the paths to literacy*. London and New York: Routledge.

Rinaldi, C. (2006). *In dialogue with Reggio Emilia: Listening, researching and learning*. London and New York: Routledge.

Smidt, S. (2013a). *Introducing Malaguzzi: A guide for practitioners and students in early years education*. London and New York: Routledge.

Gunther Kress is extremely interesting and his work is entirely readable. He is very interested in young children and their literacy development.

Culture/cultural capital/cultural competence/ cultural tools/cultural worlds

Synonymous with: Background (but very loosely)

Words or phrases linked to this concept	What it means	Why it matters
Cultural tools	The objects and signs and systems developed by humans within culture	All learners need access to the tools that allow them to make sense of their worlds
Cultural capital	What you know	Depending on who and where you are this can give you advantages in access to learning
Cultural worlds	Home is one, the neighbourhood another, school or setting a third and so on	Children are adept at operating in several cultures
Cultural competence	The ability to function well in a context	Ability to do this facilitates operating in the world
Mediation	The use of cultural tools to interpret and explain the world	What happens in all learning situations where the learning is alongside others or their ideas
Generalise a concept	To be able to put something into a category by seeing what they have in common	One of the higher order learning skills
Metacognition	Knowledge about knowledge itself	Another higher order skill
Simultaneous worlds	Children operate in more than one world which exist at the same time	A higher order skill that is not only cognitive but also social
Syncretic	Creatively transform culture	Something we all learn over time

What do you understand by the word culture? Everyone holds a common-sense definition of it that probably refers to the beliefs, artefacts, values and other things that bind people together. So when you think of your culture you might think of it in terms of the dance, music, food, language(s), religions, rituals, values, celebrations, customs and all the other things that bind you to your fellow members of that culture. This is a rather superficial definition, which ignores the roles played by the players in making culture, passing it on and changing it. By that definition culture is something fixed and 'given' to those born into it, rather than dynamic. Culture, like language, changes with usage and over time. Pinker (2002, p. 60) offers an interesting definition of culture:

The phenomena we call 'culture' arise as people pool and accumulate their discoveries and as they institute conventions to coordinate their labours and adjudicate their conflicts. When groups of people separated by time and geography accumulate different discoveries and conventions we use the plural and call them cultures.

Cultural tools are the artefacts, symbols and systems we develop within groups and use to make, share and transform meanings. They include physical tools like hoes and computers and engines and pencils and also mental or cognitive tools like books, paintings, music, alphabets, numerals. They are often specific to cultures and used to define them. You have only to think about how we talk about Chinese food, Italian cars, French style, Yiddish chutzpah or English sense of fair play to see how we take single aspects of one culture and use these to create stereotypes. You will recognise how dangerous operating with a view of certain groups of people is in terms of stereotyping and how this can lead to prejudice, discrimination, alienation and injustice.

Vygotsky said that it was through *mediation* and the use of cultural tools that children move from dependence on others and on concrete and everyday experience to be able to remember, internalise and use any experience independently. In essence what he was saying is that children move from the lower mental processes like memory, attention and intelligence to the higher functions, which are conscious.

Case study/example

These are all drawn from Karmiloff-Smith (1994) and submitted by parents who were keeping developmental diaries of their own children.

Genevieve (nineteen months): This week I gave her a bottle of juice during a meal. When she had finished I brought a second with milk. She put the two side by side and said 'two'. Other times she has simply repeated my last word but this time the 'two' was not a mimic of what I said.

(p. 174)

Genevieve is sometimes offered one thing and then another at meal times and here her mother mediates this by using the language of numbers and counting. It would seem that Genevieve, having heard the word 'two' has internalised it and used it appropriately by herself. She has heard the word, remembered it and used it on her own in a meaningful way.

Marko (thirteen months): This last week Marko has decided to push every button in the house to see what it does. If it does something, he does it again and again. He especially likes the CD player which has an 'ON' button because when he pushes it he gets a little light show.

(p. 181)

Marko, through fairly random activity (pushing buttons) has discovered that some buttons, when pressed, do something that interests and pleases him. So he repeats the actions. In order to do this he has to have generalised the concept of 'pushing buttons' and selected from this the buttons that produce a result that pleases him. Making a choice is a higher mental process.

Theo (ten months): He copied me brushing my hair the other day, and now he brushes his hair with everything brush-like, including the broom and the nailbrush. When he saw me shaving my legs this morning, he tried to help using the spoon he was holding!

(p. 185)

I love this example of a child being inducted into the practices of his mother. He watches what she does and then copies it. In doing this he has been able to compare objects and make a category of 'brush' and then select and use other types of brush in order to do what his mother has done. He has also generalised the concept of 'scraper' when he sees his mother shaving her legs (which must look like scraping them) and uses the spoon in his hand as a scraper.

Cultural capital is a concept arrived at by Bourdieu and it relates to his concerns as a Marxist sociologist about class and power. He believed that cultural capital is what we know. Each of us knows different things according to our culture. I know quite a lot about apartheid South Africa having grown up there whereas my children know a lot about England in the 1970s and beyond. This is straightforward but what is less recognised is that those children whose cultural capital is close to that of the educators and the schools and settings are more easily inducted into the culture of learning. We do, of course, through our lives acquire more cultural capital and not only acquire it but can transform what we know and value through our own learning and experience.

Cultural worlds are the different aspects of all our lives. We may see one particular culture as defining us but in reality we become members of different cultures throughout our lives. You will know that millions of children throughout the world are speakers of more than one language and many of them have to come to understand and use the symbolic systems of these different languages. Eve Gregory and her colleagues use the word *syncretic* to mean the creative transformation of culture. In this approach development is seen as a creative process where people, including children, reinvent culture, drawing on their resources, old and new. Since it refers to cross-cultural exchanges the issue of power may arise in examining the contradictions and the conflicts that arise. Speakers of languages other than English going to school in England clearly have to learn to speak, understand and deal with the host and dominant language (which is also the language of power, education, government and the media) and find ways of being able to maintain and use their home languages.

In her own words

Eve Gregory defines the principles of a syncretic approach below:

1. Children are active members of different cultural and linguistic groups and appropriating membership to a group is not a static or linear process.
2. Children do not remain in separate worlds but acquire membership of different groups simultaneously, i.e. they live in 'simultaneous worlds' (Kenner, 2003).
3. Simultaneous membership means that children syncretize the languages, literacies, narrative styles and role relationships appropriate to each group and then go on to transform the languages and cultures they use to create new forms relevant to the purpose needed.
4. Young children who participate in cross-linguistic and cross-cultural practices call upon a greater wealth of metacognitive and metalinguistic strategies. These strategies are further enhanced when they are able to *play out different roles and events*.
5. Play is a crucial feature of children's language and literacy practice with siblings, grandparents and peers.
6. The mediators, often bicultural and/or bilingual, play an essential role in early language and literacy learning. Studies investigate different forms of 'scaffolding', 'guided participation' or 'synergy' as young and older children or adults work and play together.

(Gregory et al., 2004, p. 5)

It may help you to know that metacognitive means the ability to think about thinking itself and metalinguistic is knowledge about language itself.

Cultural competence is the ability of young children to operate as full participants in the context of their culture or cultures. It is a term often used to describe how well children make sense of, create and contribute to the popular culture of their time and place.

Implications for early years practice

You, together with the children you are with, build a culture in your room, or setting or school, and the culture you create should be one that reflects and respects the diversity of languages and cultures in that setting. So you need to be conscious of the dangers of promoting one culture or set of values over another. It is important to remember that children learn through all their experiences and their learning is as valuable as the learning of the most privileged. You are in the unique position of being able to create a learning space where children can raise questions, try things out, work interactively, develop theories, use their hundred languages and fully participate.

 See also: Apprentice, bilingualism, cognitive development, decentre, ecological model, interaction with others, play, popular culture, representation and re-representation

 ## Annotated further reading

Gregory, E., Long, S. and Volk, D. (Eds) (2004). *Many pathways to literacy: Young children learning with siblings, grandparents, peers and communities*. London and New York: RoutledgeFalmer.

Karmiloff-Smith, A. (1994). *Baby, it's you*. London: Ebury Press.

Annette Karmiloff-Smith writes in two very different voices. This book was part of a TV series about child development and is written in everyday language and illustrated with delightful pictures. It is in complete contrast with her very academic book called *Beyond Modularity: A Developmental Perspective on Cognitive Science* (1995, MIT Press).

Dance:

One of the expressive arts or Hundred Languages
See also key concepts: Agency, creativity, feelings, culture, emotional development, expert others, play, representation and re-representation

Decentre

Synonymous with: See other people's point of view: not be central to everything; show empathy, theory of mind

Words or phrases linked to this concept	What it means	Why it matters
Egocentrism	Believing that you are at the centre of everything	Piaget believed that young children could not see any perspective but their own
Self-centred	Believing that you are at the centre of everything	
Show empathy	Ability to guess at what others are feelings	It is a sign of being able to decentre
Theory of mind	Ability to work out what others are feeling and to come to understand that other people have thoughts	It is a sign of being able to decentre
Prior experience	Children learn through all their previous experience	Asking children to do things where they cannot draw on any previous experience almost guarantees failure
Human sense	Where children can see the point or purpose of the activity	Where children can take on the perspectives of others because they can see why this would be important or relevant

Piaget was fond of the word *egocentrism* to describe the inability to decentre and he believed that young children were incapable of doing this. Egocentric means self-centred; to be able to decentre means to be able to adopt different perspectives or see something from the point of view of others. Yet we know that young children often *show empathy* when, for example, they comfort a friend who has fallen down or support a sibling who is in trouble. In doing this they demonstrate that they are able to work out what another person is feeling and so decentre. The same is true when children show that they can work out or guess at what people's intentions or thoughts are and this is called *theory of mind*.

Children grow up alongside others and being able to put oneself into another's shoes is essential to living and learning harmoniously in our social and cultural worlds.

Piaget who, as you know, did not consider the significance of culture, context and society to children's development, developed his idea of the egocentric child based on what is known as *The Three Mountains experiment* (Piaget and Inhelder, 1956) where he asked young children to look at a model of three mountains and select the picture that best showed the view that could be seen by a toy placed on the three-dimensional model of the mountain scenery. Children almost always chose the view that best matched what they could see. Critics of his approach, like Margaret Donaldson, said that the task was meaningless to the children, many of whom had never seen a mountain and no reason was given for choosing a particular view. In later experiments, Hughes (1975) and other researchers demonstrated that children of the same age, when asked to hide a doll or a naughty teddy from a toy policeman could do this with ease because they almost certainly had *prior experience* of hiding things, being naughty and of policemen – in real life or through stories and television. They could also see why the teddy, having done something wrong, might need to hide from the policeman so they could make what Donaldson called *human sense* of the activity.

We have arrived at two key themes in early childhood development and will define them to ensure that they are clearly understood and their significance is clear.

In our schools and settings we will have some children who have had the sort of experiences we expect them to have had – those that might be described as school-friendly. They will have had access to books and drawing materials, toys to play with, a TV or other screen to look at, outings and visits. We will almost certainly have children with very different experiences – sometimes traumatic or tragic experiences, but all the children will have something from which they learned. Some learning is evidently useful in the classroom or setting; other learning less obviously so. For all early childhood workers a recognition of previous experience – whatever it is – is essential to setting up a place of true learning, which is what your classroom or setting must be.

Case study/example

Nsamenang (Pence & Nsamenang, 2008) considers the range of childhoods possible for African children thinking about family structure, opportunities for play, the importance of peer teaching and more. Often children make their own toys from local materials. They then share these with peers who may have made their own toys. So creativity and collaboration, selection and use of available materials are part of their everyday experiences. These are cognitive skills. The children develop self-images through their families and wider culture, just as children in the developed world do. Writers like Shweder emphasise just how stimulating a childhood this can be, particularly in terms of developing pro-social behaviour. These are social skills. Often they contribute actively in the real lived life of the family and community – being out in the fields, cooking, watching the younger children, copying the older children, observing the weavers, carrying the water. These are cultural skills. They may not have access to books and screens and made toys and formal outings, but they have rich everyday experience, all of which enables them to continue to be active learners.

In their own words

Piaget said that egocentrism was:

> quite unrelated to the common meaning of the term, hypertrophy of the consciousness of self. Cognitive egocentrism, as I have tried to make clear, stems from a lack of differentiation between one's own point of view and the other possible ones, and not at all from an individualism that precedes relations with others.
>
> (Piaget, 1962, p. 4)

I wonder how easy you find it to make sense of this comment. Piaget's writing was dense and used academic or specialist language that was often deemed to be impenetrable to many readers. Try Margaret Donaldson in comparison:

> It has been claimed that children under the age of six or seven are very bad at communicating, precisely for the reason that they are bad at decentring – or that they are highly 'egocentric'. ... This claim has been made most forcibly by Jean Piaget, and it has been backed by much supporting evidence. He has made it central to his theorizing about the capacities of children in the pre-school and early school years. He has constructed such a far-reaching and closely woven net of argument, binding together so many different features of the development of behaviour, that it

is hard to believe he could be wrong. …Yet there is now powerful evidence that in this respect he is wrong.

(Donaldson, 1987, pp. 18–19)

Implications for early years practice

Piaget was extremely influential despite having many critics. You have only to look at his *stage theory* and think about how schools in the UK are structured to find evidence of this. Yet it is important not to think about young children in terms of what they cannot yet do, which is one of the tenets of his stage theory. We need to think about all the remarkable things they can do and do do. A two-year-old can walk, use her own language, handle objects and tools, take notice of other people, cry and laugh and smile and interact, express fear and love and anger and more, raise questions (often implicitly, which means not necessarily verbally but through her actions) and – most significantly – think and remember. If you still doubt that young children can decentre, just observe what happens when one child falls and cuts his knee; when a child gets into trouble for something she did not do. Living in a family in a neighbourhood, in a village or a city, all human children grow up alongside others. Being able to decentre is essential to being able to function in society.

Always have high expectations of what children are able to do if they can draw on their previous experience and make human sense of what it is they are doing.

 See also: Egocentric

Annotated further reading:

Donaldson, M. (1987). *Children's minds*. London: Fontana.

Dunn, J. (1988). *The beginnings of social understanding*. Oxford and Cambridge: Blackwell.

Halfpenny, A. and Pettersen, J. (2014). *Introducing Piaget: A guide for practitioners and students in early years education*. London and New York: Routledge.

Margaret Donaldson's book is a classic and you should all read it if you have not already. It is very accessible, relevant and enlightening.

Judy Dunn studied social development within families and her book is also very readable and full of treats.

Developmentally Appropriate Practice (DAP)

Synonymous with: Self-initiated/directed play

Words or phrases linked to this concept	What it means	Why it matters
The lived lives	The day-to-day ordinary lives of people	People always live in a context and the context matters
Individualism	Promoting the notion of the child as an individual rather than as a member of society	No child is without people around her. All learning takes place in a context and culture
Self-initiated and self-directed play	In the developed world we promote the idea of children learning through play	In reality children also learn through their lived lives, through narrative and through interactions
Richly resourced environment	It would be lovely if we could all have this but the reality is different	Children learn and develop wherever they are, using what is at hand
Ideal/model child	Find me one!	All children are different
Good parent	Who can define this? According to whose values and culture and economic situation?	

DAP arose out of a programme in the United States relating to the quality of childcare. It is a guide which assumes that both parents and carers know relatively little about children and offers detailed and prescriptive advice about what to do at each age and stage of a child's life. The first edition was published in 1987 and was criticised on the basis of being more or less context-free and operating on the basis of all children being more or less the same. The main arguments came from those in the field who were concerned about how little it related to the *lived lives* of millions of children – those not part of the perceived model group – i.e. not white, English speaking, middle class, and living with two parents. A second edition was published in 1997 and it eradicated some of the more offensive exclusions but still focused on the Western model of an ideal family with an ideal child living in ideal surroundings.

The programme emphasises *individualism* and pays scant attention to some of the characteristics of children like helpfulness and cooperation, which those in developing countries might use as markers of growing maturity and cognitive development. So it is based still on a Piagetian model of the solo scientist seeking to make meaning in a richly resourced setting. The emphasis of DAP in this country is largely on *self-initiated and self-directed play*, which are said to be the most effective ways of learning and need to take place in a *richly resourced environment* and offered by trained teachers. Play is vital in the early years, but so is the ability to listen and to look and to question and to use the hundred languages. Play is one mode of learning but not the only one. Viruru, who writes powerfully about inequalities, says that a huge amount of what is written about early childhood education and care is written in the language of privilege and influence. It is as far removed from the realities of the lives of so many children and predicated on a level of material resourcing impossible for the majority of the world's children.

One of the worst aspects of the DAP is the underpinning idea of this *model child* in a model family because it has given rise to a host of initiatives to train parents in parenting. Who decides what makes a *good parent*? Can a parent be poor and good or is it only those with resources who can be good parents? Can a parent be black or non-English speaking or have a disability or be gay and be a good parent? Is my idea of a good parent the same as yours?

It is essential for all of us involved in the lives of young children and their families that we understand and respect that there are many different ways of seeing childhood.

Case study/example

Alma Gottlieb studied the lives of infants in a Beng village in West Africa. They are a minority group in Cote d'Ivoire with a powerful belief in what they call *wrugbe*, which means the afterlife. Just to give a sense of how great differences can be, here is what Gottlieb herself says:

> One day I was sitting in the shaded compound of a Beng village in the West African rain forest, playing 'This Little Piggy' with the toes of six-month-old Amwe. As the last little piggy went home, I laughed aloud at myself. The baby could not possibly understand the words of the nursery rhyme, all the more because they were in English. To my amazement, Amwe's mother, my friend Amenan, objected strongly to my remark, which she took as an insult to her daughter. Amenan herself understood not a word of English – although she spoke six languages. Nevertheless, Amenan insisted that Amwe understood my ditty perfectly well. Curious but somewhat skeptical, I asked, 'You think so?' Amenan invoked the afterlife. Unlike life in this world, she pointed out, in the Beng afterlife – called *wrugbe* – all peoples of the world live harmoniously and are fluent in all languages. But how did this result in her infant daughter's purported ability to understand 'This Little Piggy' in English? Patiently, Amenan explained: Babies are reincarnations of ancestors, and they have just come from *wrugbe*. Having just lived elsewhere, they remember much from that other world – including the many languages spoken by its residents.

In order to answer the question she had just raised, Gottlieb studied childrearing within this group of people and wrote an influential book *The Afterlife is Where We Come From* (2004). She found that babies were seen as part of the group not as individuals. They represent insurance against old age and share in household and daily tasks. When they play, they play with what is at hand but they have many playmates. They are trained by the adults to take responsibility for running errands and looking after younger children. This training is often gendered with boys and girls performing different tasks. But it is a culture of shared meanings and peer influence.

In her own words

Helen Penn writes with passion about the difficulties of operating within the framework of traditional child development. Here is what she says:

> Child development is a discipline that argues we should focus on young children; we should not neglect them because they are such an important part of life. To ignore the specifics of children's lives would be like ignoring the specifics of women's lives in giving an account of society. As a discipline it is unique and important, and without it our understanding of others would be very limited. But child development is also a discipline that has been forged in a Euro-American context, making use implicitly of common societal assumptions, and drawing on a very narrow evidence base. Despite its subject matter, it can distort and distract, as much as enhance our understanding of the unequal lives that so many children live.
>
> (Penn, 2005, pp. 64–65)

Implications for early years practice

Plan for real and different children from real and different families with real and different experiences. Do not operate on the notion that there is only one way of doing things. If someone tells you that children must learn through play, smile and decide for yourself if play is the only mode of learning. Challenge anyone who tells you they know what makes a good parent. Think carefully about what you know about the children and if there are gaps in your knowledge do your best to fill them. Know and respect the children and value what they bring.

 See also: Complex environments

Annotated further reading:

Penn, H. (2005). *Unequal childhoods: Young children's lives in poor countries*. London and New York: Routledge.

Dialogic education:

Where the learner and teacher are equal partners in any exchange and where the learner is not an empty vessel or a blank slate
See also key concepts: Agency, asking questions, cognitive development, expert others, first-hand, guided participation, identity, imitation, inclusion, interaction, meaning, popular culture, relationship

Divergent thinking:

Thinking in a novel or unusual way
See also key concepts: Asking questions, creativity

Documenting children's progress

Synonymous with: Recording, record-keeping, observing learning, co-constructor of children's culture

Words or phrases linked to this concept	What it means	Why it matters
Co-constructor of children's culture	Term used in Reggio Emilia to explain the importance of adults documenting what children do	It is part of the collaboration between adults and children in building a portrait of each child's progress
Key worker	The person with prime responsibility for any particular child	Having a special adult attached to you helps build the child's confidence and aids settling easily into the setting
Starting point	Sometimes called baseline this is the essential information to be gathered prior to or on entry	Allows everyone who is to know the child get to know essential things about her experience and more
Observation notes	What the adults do as they observe the children	Essential to getting to know how the child is progressing in all aspects of learning and development
Visible listening	Vecchi's term for children monitoring their own and their peers' progress using digital cameras	A very collaborative approach to recognising that children can monitor their own progress and that of others
Biographical narrative	The story of a child's life in the class or setting	

In the UK many adults regard the requirement to keep records of children's progress as some sort of imposition from those in authority. And, of course, if the purpose of the record is not clear or agreed by all those involved it will feel like an add-on rather than like an essential ingredient in the child's learning and development. I am absolutely certain that the only way to ensure that you are doing the best for each child is to watch them, listen to them, record what you hear and see, think about what it tells you about what the child already knows, can do and is interested in and use that to plan what to do next. It becomes a cycle and it needs to be shared with those involved – all the adults, the children themselves and their parents and carers. And you need to do it for babies, for toddlers and for all the children in your care. They do this in all the best early years provision I have seen here, in Reggio Emilia and elsewhere.

Another table, this time to show you what adults need to do, what sort of information they might gather and why. In Reggio Emilia they talk of this as the adult being a *co-constructor of children's culture*.

What needs doing	What information is needed	What is the purpose
Any adult who seeks to be a co-constructor of children's culture must, above all, keep detailed documents that will be built into a complex story about each individual child	As an introduction, as much information as can be gathered about the child's experiences prior to entry and about the aspects of the child's culture that are significant Regularly, all the notes that have been made about the child's engagement in the setting – her interests, her relationships, her responses Examples of what the child has said and done, all dated and often annotated	Like an archaeologist, the educator scrutinises her daily findings about individual children and over time constructs these into a detailed, individual account of the child's development

Documenting a child's development as a learner is one of the most crucial aspects of being an educator. Through observation the teacher or practitioner becomes able to say how each one learns and interacts, raises questions and develops theories, can share and support, and behave and relate to one another.

Case study/example

First is an example of the information collected by a child's *key worker* when he started in the setting. This information will be the starting point for the life story that will develop over his time in the nursery. His parents are Turkish speakers and they were spoken to by the nursery teacher and a translator from the local Turkish community.

> Ozman is three years old. He is the oldest child in the family, His sister Zeynep is two years old and the baby is only just born. The family have lived in this area since they came to London in 2013. Dad works for his brother who has a restaurant on the high street so he works long hours and is often too late home to see much of the children. Mum is home all day but she speaks no English although she is just starting to go to a class at the school where Ozman is enrolled. Ozman has a little English because his cousin is older and they play together but at home he speaks Turkish. He loves to play with cars and anything with wheels; watches TV a lot and loves games on his mum's phone. He loves sorting things out and spends lots of time doing this.

So we know a little bit about Ozman and his family and this gives us and the nursery workers a foundation on which to build.

Now we look at the *observation notes* made by the teaching assistant in the nursery, who is Ozman's key worker and herself a Turkish speaker. She has been observing Ozman playing in the home corner. Here are her notes:

> O is in the home corner with Leonardo and Julia. He is pretending to cook and tells Julia to set the table. She asks who is there for tea. He says 'three' and points to himself, Leonardo and Julia. Julia gets three of each – cup and saucer and puts them on the table. O says 'Not right' and moves them around so that each cup sits on a saucer of the same colour. 'Better' he says. Leonardo tells Julia to bake the cake. She says she can't bake. O gets a bowl and a spoon and makes a lot of noise bashing the bowl with the spoon. 'Cake' he says and smiles.

Later Zohra, the teaching assistant, sits down with the class teacher to go through the day's observation notes for a small group of children. After a discussion Zohra writes this at the bottom of the observation note:

> Date ... 9/4/2013
> O in home corner used English with confidence. Only a few words but certainly communicating. He is joining in pretend play for the first time. Will read 'Tiger Who Came to Tea' to his group tomorrow.

At the end of the first term Ozman gets a note to take home to his mum and dad, written in both English and Turkish. It says:

> Ozman has had a very successful first term in the nursery. When he came he spoke very little English, was shy and found it difficult to join in. But now he is really enjoying school. He has made friends and loves playing in the home corner and story time where he is now able to follow the story, especially when we leave the book out with the story props so he can re-tell the story with his friends. He can count to 20 and is beginning to write some words that he knows – mainly the names of his friends.

This is all rather straightforward and you must be wondering what there is to learn from this. So let me entertain you with some of the more in-depth and sophisticated records kept by the workers in the Reggio Emilia pre-schools. They use cameras as well as written records. They have the resources to document some of their special projects in the form of books they publish in-house. They make regular displays of what the children have been doing and saying and ensure that parents are able to come and see these. Where there are babies the staff put up each day for the parents or carers a record of what the baby did. This is important because a parent needs to know if the baby has had a sleep and when; or a meal and when. And working parents will regret missing those significant moments – the first word, the first step. Vea Vecchi writes about *visible listening*, a term that I find fascinating and revealing. What this means is involving the children themselves in documenting what they and their friends do by using digital cameras. I am not suggesting giving yourself additional work and stress. This is fine where there are resources and staff in abundance, but the principle is important. Educators need to know what children know, can do and are interested in to ensure that they offer activities to meet their needs. Parents and carers need to know what children have been doing and be treated as partners in this enterprise of the education and care of young children.

In her own words

Rinaldi says:

> Documentation offers the teacher a unique opportunity to re-listen, re-see and re-visit, both individually and with others, the events and processes in which she was the co-protagonist, either directly or indirectly.
>
> Documentation is a fundamental support for the self-evaluation, and the group evaluation of the theories and hypotheses of each child.

Documentation provides an extraordinary opportunity for parents, as it gives them the possibility to know not only what their child is doing, but also the how and why, the meaning that the child gives to what he does, and the shared meanings with other children.

(Rinaldi, 2006 pp. 58–59)

Implications for early years practice

Documenting what children do and what you do in response is one of the most important aspects of your work but you do need to remain realistic and not try to do everything. The model of Reggio Emilia is wonderful but remember that its practitioners are well resourced, whereas you may not be in your setting or school. Try to work out a system that suits your way of working.

Here are some ideas given to me by students, teachers, teaching assistants and others:

- Carry a notebook and jot down things that attract your attention.
- Date everything.
- Make time each day to observe one or two children or one or two groups and here make more detailed notes.
- Develop your own brand of shorthand. Everyone does this differently.
- Make sure you read your notes the same day or you will not be able to make sense of them.
- Keep everything. Date everything.
- Start a folder for each child in your group or for whom you are key worker.
- Use cameras – the one on your phone will be fine.
- Comment on what children say, who they are with, if they talk, ask questions, suggest theories.
- Notice their physical skills.
- Note anything that strikes you about their social and emotional development.
- Keep bits of writing, drawing, mark-making.
- Work with your colleagues: all the adults should play an equal part in this process of documentation.
- Anything, anywhere, that seems significant should be recorded. So lunch times, story time, playtimes, PE times, on outings.
- Create a biographical narrative for each child as a whole person learning in all situations, through all interactions and encounters.

See also: Interaction with others, scaffolding learning

Annotated further reading:

Rinaldi (2006) and Vecchi (2010) have been mentioned before, are both readable and fascinating but perhaps a little off-putting in view of the hard-won and now plentiful resources available to practitioners in Reggio Emilia.

Smidt, S. (due 2014). *Observing, assessing and planning for children in the early years.* (2nd edn). London and New York: Routledge and Nursery World.

This book in its first edition is out of date. It was designed to help practitioners in England consider how to plan for learning and document to illustrate learning.

Drawing:

expressing ideas or feelings graphically through making images, using colour, line, texture, pattern

See also key concepts: Collaboration, complex environments, creativity, documenting progress, meaning, mark-making and monologues

Ecological model

Synonymous with: Bionomics

Words or phrases linked to this concept	What it means	Why it matters
Ecological	The interactions between living things and their environment	It allows us to consider everything that affects individuals and groups
Microsystem	What affects the person in the most intimate of environments	How the child is affected by home, neighbourhood, school, etc.
Mesosystem	What affects the person in the system just beyond the home	How the child is affected by the links between home and mosque, home and creche, etc.
Exosystem	What affects the person more remotely	How the child is affected by more remote systems like parent's place of work
Macrosystem	What affects the person significantly but not close to	How the child is affected by things like laws and economics systems, the media and more
Chronosystem	The outermost layer referring to time	What impacts on an individual will be directly related to that individual's age
Construction of identity	What the child does in order to develop and adapt her sense of herself	This is a dynamic process requiring social and cognitive skills
Dialects	A language within a language, related to regions	
Discourse	A fancy word for written or spoken communication	

The word *ecology* simply means the interactions between organisms, including human beings, and their environment.

Urie Bronfenbrenner (1979) was one of the first theorists to examine the intersecting worlds of children through his 'ecological' model. His original version consisted of four concentric circles named the *microsystem*, the *mesosystem*, the *exosystem* and the *macrosystem*. You will see how this model works with the individual child at its centre and then the concentric circles, one within the other, to show the movement from the most intimate contexts of the home to the more remote contexts beyond. So the innermost circle, the microsystem, represents the everyday context of the life of young children, which is usually the home but may move beyond into the extended family, the neighbourhood and perhaps the crèche or the nursery setting. The next circle represents what is known as the mesosystem and these are seen to be the links between home and clinic, home and church or mosque or synagogue, between home and nursery or school and so on. More remote yet are things that affect the child more indirectly and these are called the exosystem and include things like community networks and the workplace of the parents, perhaps. Finally, and most remote from the child but still impacting on her life, is the macrosystem, which is where social systems like laws and economics and the media and the education system make decisions that affect the child and his or her family. You can see how the child's cultures come together through this model. As you can see for our purposes, the child, labelled 'you', is at the centre of the concentric circles.

The diagram below is Bronfenbrenner's revised version, that refers also to time, which forms the fifth circle labelled *chronosystem*.

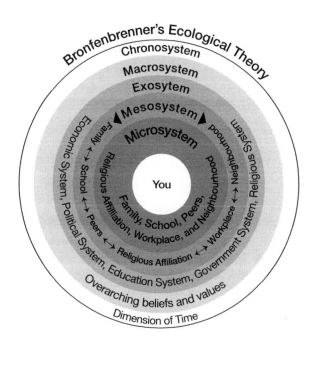

Within each of their cultural groups children set about defining themselves as members of that group, using the cultural tools available to them to define their family roles, gender roles, images, languages, in their complex worlds. This, the *construction of identity*, is one of the earliest tasks for the human infant. Neither identity nor culture is fixed but are dynamic and fluid, relational and relative concepts. So the identity of the child at home is not one thing, but might be baby or sibling or competent or difficult according to circumstance and context.

Case study/example

> Masha is very quiet and withdrawn when her Uncle Leo visits. He is a big and noisy man and he terrifies her. But when he leaves she returns to being her cheerful and outgoing self.
>
> Henry is the older sibling and is expected to be grown-up and sensible and responsible. Usually he is but every so often he loses his temper and resorts to stamping his feet and shrieking like a two-year-old.
>
> Constructing identity is a complex thing to have to do, particularly constructing many identities according to context. The child at home may be very different from the child at school and we know that in order to construct self-images in new contexts the child has to come to know which cultural tools are available and use these in order to become part of that context. So children need to make sense of a wide range of things including language or languages, relevant dialects and registers; discourse or discourses, which are ways of speaking and acting; religious practices and belief systems; values and norms including knowing what is acceptable and what not; and customs that can include ways of eating, dressing, speaking, gazing, interacting and learning. So within their separate and their intersecting cultures children learn the relevant tools and sometimes encounter conflicts and dichotomies.
>
> (Based on Smidt, 2013a)

In his own words

Bronfenbrenner was a Russian American psychologist and has gained a reputation as one of the foremost scholars examining the interplay between research and policy on child development. He had a firm belief in the necessity for science to be supported by policy and policy underpinned by science.

> Children need people in order to become human. ... It is primarily through observing, playing, and working with others older and younger than himself that

a child discovers both what he can do and who he can become – that he develops both his ability and his identity. ... Hence to relegate children to a world of their own is to deprive them of their humanity, and ourselves as well.

(Bronfenbrenner, 1973, Preface)

 ## *Implications for early years practice*

This serves as a reminder that we live in a social world and that all learning is set in a context and a culture. You may find it interesting to think about how all the children you encounter will have constructed a particular identity for the class or setting which may be very different from the identity created for the home or the playground. This will help you take seriously the different ways of behaving or talking, the expressed interests and the styles of interacting you observe. It helps us all take popular culture and its role in the lives of children seriously.

 See also: Culture

 ## *Annotated further reading:*

Smidt, S. (2013a). *Introducing Malaguzzi: A guide for practitioners and students in early years education*. London and New York: Routledge.

Egocentric

Synonymous with: Self-centred, unable to decentre, see things from own perspective

Words or phrases linked to this concept	What it means	Why it matters
Perceptual egocentrism	A child believing that everyone can see what she can see	If this were so it would show that children were not actively making meaning
Communicative egocentrism	The inability of the young child to recognise that an absent person cannot see gestures or expression	Another deficit view of the young infant
Egocentric speech	Speech not directed at other people in Piaget's definition. For Vygotsky all speech is social	For Piaget the first speech was autistic
Inner speech	The speech that is not heard – i.e. thought	The result of outer speech having become internalised
Outer speech	The speech that is heard – i.e. verbalising	Saying things out loud
Monologues	Synonymous with egocentric speech or outer speech	Very significant in cognitive development
Consciously	To do something with intent and understanding, aware of what you are doing	Very significant in cognitive development
Internalised	When something is absorbed so that the learner does not need physical props or spoken language	Very significant in cognitive development

Egocentrism was a central tenet of Piaget's analysis of how young children learn. He believed that they were not able to see the perspectives of others. In this sense he was not seeing young children as self-centred or self-absorbed, but rather as only able to think in terms of putting themselves at the centre of any event.

Piaget talked about *perceptual egocentrism*, which focused on the idea that young children assume that everyone, from whatever viewpoint, sees what the child herself sees. As you may know, this view has been challenged by Donaldson and Hughes on the basis of Piaget not having considered the significance of the child being able to draw on prior experience and to see the purpose of the given activity.

He also talked of *communicative egocentrism* where children talk to themselves or to others without realising that these others do not have access to what is in the child's mind. Halfpenny and Pettersen cite the example of the child talking on the phone to her dad and shaking her head when asked, by dad, if mum is there. Piaget's analysis of this is that the fact that dad is not able to see her gesture does not matter. I am not sure that this explanation matches my idea of the competent, meaning-making child.

Piaget also talked of *egocentric speech*, which he saw as needing neither an audience nor a listener. The child talks out loud for the pure satisfaction of doing so. But for Vygotsky all speech was social in the sense that it was always about communicating with others. So when Vygotsky talked of egocentric speech he saw it as the transition from *outer speech* to *inner speech*. In short what this means is that first children need to verbally express what they are doing or thinking. That is egocentric speech. When the child no longer needs to vocalise thought the egocentric speech has been internalised. So the outer speech has become inner speech.

Let us think a little more about children talking out loud to themselves without any need of an audience. Another term for this is monologue. You will surely have heard young children doing this – often when they are alone in their cots at night or in their prams in the garden or lying on a rug under a tree. They engage in monologues, repetitions, comments on life and experiences. While for Piaget there was no social basis for this, for Vygotsky there was. Nonetheless he accepted Piaget's definition and felt that this egocentric speech offered a window into the processes operating during the silent, what one might call 'speech-for-oneself' phase on the road to the verbal thinking that is so evident in older children and adults.

Case study/example

> A four-year-old child was trying to reach some candy, placed too high for her to reach. The child talked herself through the problem as she solved it. This monologue or outer speech clearly accompanied her actions. Speech and problem solving came together in the child's running commentary. As she climbed on the divan and jumped up she said, 'That candy is up so high … I have to call Mommy so she will get it for me. There's no way I can reach it, it's so high.' She then picked up a stick and looked at the candy, saying, 'Papa has a big cupboard and sometimes he can reach things.' When she accomplished the task and used the stick to knock the sweets off the shelf she laughed and announced, 'There. The stick got it. I'll have to take this stick home with me.'
>
> (Cited in Luria, 1976; text amendments responsibility of Smidt, 2009)

It is only when this outer speech becomes *internalised* (which means it may no longer be spoken or evident to anyone other than the child) that the child uses it privately, internally and *consciously* to solve problems. Here is an example drawn from the work of Kenner (2004).

She describes how Yazan experimented with the directionality of print in English and Arabic. Asked by one of his peers to write his name in English, he

> attempted to write it using Arabic directionality, going from right to left instead of left to right. Kenner suggests that he seemed to be asking himself (using internalised speech) 'What happens if you write English from right to left?'. On another occasion he wrote his sister's name in English script with the first name going from right to left and the second name from left to right.
>
> (p. 97)

In his own words

Bruner writes a wonderful description of his view of Piaget's growing child and the world he lived in:

> He is virtually alone in it, a world of objects that he must array in space, time and causal relationships. He begins his journey egocentrically and must impose properties on the world that will eventually be shared with others. But others give him little help. The social reciprocity of infant and mother plays a very small role in Piaget's account of development. And language gives neither hints nor even a means of unravelling the puzzles of the world to which language applies. Piaget's child has one overwhelming problem: to bring the inner representations of mind into equilibrium with the structures of experience. Piaget's children are little intellectuals, detached from the hurly-burly of the human condition.
>
> (1983, p. 138)

I love this picture of the tireless and lonely explorer, not able to seek or use the support of others, isolated in his search for meaning. I love the brilliance of the portrait but this is not the meaning-making, questioning, creative and social child of my experience.

Implications for early years practice

It is interesting to think about egocentricity and its implications but in terms of practice what seems significant to me is to remember, always, the vital role played by others – adults and children – in the lives and learning of babies and children. The more opportunities and activities you offer that invite and allow children to share and discuss, try things out, help one another, talk through what they are doing or just observe one another, the more pleasure you will get in watching the learning that happens before your very eyes. One of the most pleasing things about being involved in the learning of young children is what you learn from watching them and listening to them, always alert for what they know and can do rather than what they do not know and cannot do yet.

See also: Decentre

 Annotated further reading:

Bruner, J. (1983). *Child's talk: Learning to use language*. Oxford: Oxford University Press

Kenner, C. (2004). *Becoming biliterate: Young children learning different writing systems*. Stoke on Trent and Sterling, USA: Trentham Books.

Halfpenny, A. and Pettersen, J. (2014). *Introducing Piaget: A guide for practitioners and students in early years education*. London and New York: Routledge.

Smidt, S. (2009). *Introducing Vygotsky: A guide for practitioners and students in early years education*. London and New York: Routledge.

Bruner, again, quite difficult to read but worth the effort. Kenner's book is a straightforward and very readable account of her work and her intense interest in the learning of bilingual children.

Egocentric speech:

Speaking aloud whilst doing something
Synonymous with: External speech
See also key concepts: Egocentric, monologues

Emotional development

Synonymous with: Affective development

Words or phrases linked to this concept	What it means	Why it matters
Emotional literacy	The ability to understand and handle your own emotions	Being able to handle emotions is important for all aspects of development
Emotional capital	The social and cultural resources generated through affective or emotional relationships, usually within the family	It can be seen as an investment in others, particularly in the education of others
Dispositions	A tendency to show often, consciously and voluntarily a pattern of behaviour that is goal-directed	A term used by Lilian Katz to indicate a tendency to respond in particular ways

Thinking in everyday or real-life terms you will all appreciate what emotional development entails when you think about the helplessness and dependence of the newborn infant and then of the fierce independence of mind of the five-year-old. The young child has to learn to be less and less dependent on the help and support of others. She has to learn to live in her family and community, which involves her learning her language in order to share her thoughts and ideas and feelings. She must learn also what the thoughts and ideas and feelings of others are so that she can empathise with them and feel their joy or sorrow, anger or delight, fear and wonder and much more. On this journey the child has to learn to express and control and channel her feelings. If she does not they could overwhelm her.

As always with academic writing new terms are created to either clarify or muddy the waters. One of these terms is *emotional literacy*, which is sometimes said to mean the same thing as emotional intelligence although some people think the two are different. Claude Steiner (1997) says that it is made up of the ability to understand emotions, listen to others and empathise with their emotions and express emotions productively. To be emotionally literate is to be able to handle emotions in a way that improves your personal power and improves the quality of life around you. Emotional literacy is said to improve relationships, create loving possibilities between people, make cooperative work possible and facilitate the feeling of community. Steiner, coming from a counselling background, states that he sees emotion in a social and interactive context but there is a strand of negativity in it. In summary he believes that emotional literacy involves developing a sense of empathy, to manage one's own emotion, the ability to repair emotional damage and the facility for putting this all together, which he calls emotional interactivity. This worries me in some ways because the emphasis is on the individual and in this sense is inward looking and not really social or interactive.

A great deal of what is written about emotional development focuses on the negative. Think of what you have read about dealing with temper tantrums, anger management, inability to share, inability to concentrate, unable to take turns, difficulties in socialising. It is as though we expect children to show only the behaviours that please us and are easy to handle. Lilian Katz, an American writer and researcher, considered *dispositions* (or habits of mind) as very significant in learning and development, closely related to feelings. Anxiety is a feeling, curiosity a disposition; fear is a feeling, being bossy is a disposition; loneliness is a feeling, being interested in learning is a disposition. Katz suggested that adults engaged with young children who support or praise or encourage a disposition strengthen it in the child.

Case study/example

Unusually, the example offered here is Diane McClellan and Lilian Katz's (2001) checklist on what to look out for when considering the emotional and social development of young children rather than a case study.

- *Range of affect* – look out for children displaying a range of appropriate emotions like sorrow, pleasure, anger and excitement. A child seeming to display one or two emotions over and over again would suggest you need to find out why.
- *Variations in play* – look out for whether or not the child plays in the same way with the same things or whether the child is open to trying new things. Responding to change suggests a child is beginning to be able to manipulate the environment.
- *Curiosity* – look out to see if a child displays curiosity about new things or changes. You can spot curiosity when the child pays attention to something, asks questions or even does something forbidden. Taking risks is an essential part of learning.
- *Acceptance of authority* – look for an appropriate acceptance of authority where the child usually does what is asked but sometimes refuses by having a tantrum or just not joining in.
- *Friendship* – look out for the child being able to initiate, maintain and enjoy relationships with one or more children. Of course children may sometimes want to be alone but you are looking for growing social confidence.
- *Interest* – look out for the child to sometimes get deeply involved in something.
- *Spontaneous affect* – look out for the child demonstrating spontaneous signs of affection towards family members or others. You are wanting to see that the child loves and knows that she is loved and responds to this appropriately.

In his own words

I want to offer you a new voice, that of the Greek educationalist Alexandros K. Kakavoulis, who presents a very positive and life-affirming view of aspects of emotional development in young children. You will find this very readable.

Research has revealed that long before children receive any formal moral or religious education from their parents or school, they have the ability to empathise, that is to know what another person is feeling. Infants, for instance, of one-year-old, cry when they hear other babies crying, and while some claim that this is just emotional copying, sharing feelings may actually be the first step toward mature empathy

(Radke-Yarrow et al., 1983). At the same age infants are often 'sharing' interesting experiences by pointing, and they will occasionally offer toys to their companions (Hay, 1979; Leung & Rheingold, 1981). By the age of one, some children are already ready to help with household chores, such as sweeping, dusting, or setting the table (Rheingold, 1982).

Two-year-old toddlers may bring a teddy bear to a distressed child, and if that does not help, they will try something else. They sympathise, bring someone else to help, and try to change the other's sad feelings (Radke-Yarrow et al., 1983; Zahn-Waxler & Radke-Yarrow, 1982). At the age of two-to-three, children spontaneously give gifts and share their toys with other children and with unfamiliar adults (Stanjek, 1978). Helping behaviour begins at this age too. Children will stop what they are doing to clear an obstacle from another's path and help each other clean up spilled puzzles and the like. On the whole, empathy for other children in distress, cooperation with others to achieve common goals, and helping someone else to do something all increase during the pre-school years (Bar-Tal et al., 1982; Hart et al., 1992; Marcus et al., 1979).

Individual differences in altruistic behaviour have been found too. Some children show more of these positive behaviours than others (Murphy, 1992), and the tendency for some of them to be more benevolent than others seems to be stable over time: Four-years-olds who were generous, cooperative, empathic, considerate, and helpful were found to be the same at the age of five. Children who are socially responsible in nursery school are still behaving more responsibly than their peers five to six years later (Eisenberg, 1992).

Whether a child is first- or later-born and comes from a socioeconomic advantaged or disadvantaged family, and is a boy or a girl does not seem to affect altruistic behaviour. The qualities that make a difference, sociability, happiness, assertiveness and adjustment. Children who are interested in being with others offer help more than shy children; and those who laugh and smile often help more than children who show positive emotions less often. Those children who defend their own needs are more likely to help spontaneously. In contrast, timid children tend to help only when asked, perhaps because they want to avoid conflict. Finally, altruistic children are generally well adjusted and good at coping with stress. As Eisenberg concludes 'children with strong prosocial dispositions tend to be emotionally expressive, socially skilled, assertive and well adjusted' (Eisenberg, 1992, p. 43).

Three major explanations have been offered to explain why some children are more altruistic than others. Answers to this question have come from three major theoretical approaches: attachment, cognitive, and social learning theories.

Research has shown that social skills are indeed better developed in children who had secure attachments. In one study, three-/four-year-olds who had been securely attached were the ones other children wanted to play with. They were less withdrawn, more likely to be leaders, and more sympathetic to their peers' distress than pre-schoolers who had been judged insecure as infants (Kestenbaum, Farber & Sroufe, 1989).

For cognitive theorists, empathy and altruistic behaviour are linked to perspective taking. As children's egocentrism (according to Piaget's notion) lessens and perspective-taking capacities grow, their altruistic behaviours increase. 'Doing the right thing' increases, too, as children learn to identify what others are actually feeling (Cassidy et al., 1992). This kind of sensitivity is enhanced when parents speak to their children about feelings such as sadness, anger, happiness, jealousy, during the pre-school years (Dunn, Brown & Beardsall, 1991).

For social learning theorists, altruism can result from imitation. In one study, pre-school children who had observed an adult model sharing, helping, and being sympathetic, acted more like that themselves 2 weeks later, than children who had not seen such a model (Yarrow et al., 1973). And the effects of more extensive modelling seem to endure beyond several days and sometimes even several months (Radke-Yarrow et al., 1983). Children are also reinforced for being sympathetic and for sharing, helping, and cooperating by being praised with phrases such as 'That's a good girl'; 'You're a nice boy'; 'Thank you for helping'.

(Kakavoulis, 1998, pp. 115–126)

 ## Implications for early years practice

There is a huge amount you can read about emotional development and you need to know that this is just a very small taster. Many theorists see close links between cognitive and emotional behaviour. Others adopt a softer and somewhat sentimentalised view. The dominating voice is, however, still somewhat negative. What I am urging in this section is that you pay attention to what children are doing, saying, representing and asking and from this make some assessment of how well they are doing as young children trying to make sense of this intensely complex world. You will find that most of them are competent and questioning and able to feel a range of emotions. More than that they can adapt their behaviour to the norms of their cultures and work out what others are thinking and feeling. They are as emotionally competent as they are cognitively competent, even in the face of difficulties. Be alert to how poverty, ill health, lack of access to facilities, alienation and prejudice may, of course, affect their emotional development but in my experience, most young children are resilient and strong once they are able to establish relationships with others.

 See also: Cognitive development, documenting children's progress, feelings

📖 *Annotated further reading:*

Kakavoulis, A. K. (1998). Early childhood altruism: How parents see prosocial behaviour in their young children. *Early Child Development and Care, 140*(1), 115–126, DOI: 10.1080/0300443981400109

McClellan, D. E., & Katz, L. G. (2001). Assessing young children's social competence. *ERIC Digest* [online]. Available at: http://ericeece.org/pubs/digests/2001/mcclel01.html

Both these readings are journal articles. The first one is in the journal called *Early Child Development and Care* and the second in the *Eric Digest* online.

Expectations:

The ways in which you plan or evaluate according to what you believe the child is capable of
See also key concepts: Attention, cognitive development, decentre, feelings, interaction with others, narrative

Expert others

Synonymous with: Experienced learners

Words or phrases linked to this concept	What it means	Why it matters
Peer teaching	Where a more expert child teaches another incidentally or through a planned interaction	Children interact with and learn from one another all the time. During their interactions they not only learn but share their experience – hence they teach
Reciprocal teaching	A learning situation where there is some explicit teaching but where there is more turn taking	The underpinning pedagogy is that of inviting children to ask questions and be active learners
Biliterate	Able to read and write two or more languages	In reality children are called biliterate when they know something about the writing of their culture. They do not have to be fluent readers or writers for the term to be applied to them
Metacognitive skills	Knowing what you know	A higher order learning skill
Dialogic education	Where teacher and learner respect one another, engage in dialogue and swap roles	Most early childhood education is based on this model, although the demands of too early formal teaching are threatening this
Side-by-side reading	Children looking at books alongside one another	Some settings set up time when children can just sit beside one another and look at books
Significant moments	The first time the child does something	Try to always record these in some way as they mark the steps in learning and development

An expert other is someone who is more expert, has had more experience and knows more than a less experienced or less expert other. Vygotsky, in his sociocultural analysis, talked of how the child's experience of the world is mediated through her interactions with others who are more experienced or expert. In the thinking of the day more expert others were assumed to be adults, but Vygotsky made the extremely important point that children learn from one another. A child who has more experience of being in the class or setting knows more about what is expected in that setting and is thus the more expert other. The same child may know less about how to make stable sandcastles than the newcomer to the setting and so the roles are swapped. You will see that the status of each learner in any exchange may change according to the context.

The terms *peer teaching* and *reciprocal teaching* can be used to describe the intentional or unintentional situations where children learn and teach together.

Case study/example

The first study comes from the work of Kenner who invited six-year-old biliterate children to share their growing understandings about how the written language of their culture works. This is peer teaching in action.

> Tala decided to teach Emily to write a word in Arabic – a language with which Emily was not familiar. The word she wanted to teach Emily to write was the name of her brother Khalid. In Arabic this is is written in two parts, 'Kha' and 'lid' because, according to the rules of Arabic writing, the letters 'alif' (which represent the 'a' sound) cannot join to any following letter. Tala wrote the word herself, in front of Emily, telling her what she was doing.
>
> [...] 'Do that – it's like a triangle, but it's got a line like here … go 'wheee' like this (as she finished with an upward stroke). Emily tried to follow this lead, saying as she wrote 'It looks like an "L" … it looks like steps.' … Emily was interpreting an unfamiliar script from the basis of English and of visual images. However, Tala realised that Emily had over-interpreted her instructions, with the result being too stylised and she commented 'It's not exactly like that – she's done steps'. Indeed, Emily's version looked like steps in a staircase rather than the fluid curves typical of Arabic writing. This difficulty continued during the lesson and to help her friend produce more appropriate writing, Tala resorted to a technique used by her own Arabic teacher. She provided a 'join-the-dots' version of the words required.
>
> (Kenner, 2004, p. 113)

Do you see how fluently Tala steps into the role of teacher? She knows that she knows more about what she is teaching Emily than Emily does and so she automatically adopts the stance, the tone of voice and even the pedagogic device she has seen in her teachers. Through her interactions with the more expert other of the teacher she has learned something about pedagogy.

The second example illustrates reciprocal teaching and come from my own observation notes.

> Six-year-old Cass wants to know how to work out the concept 'goes into'. Her sister, whilst they were playing school, told her to learn this and so she has asked her teacher. The teacher says, 'Let's start with some blocks to help us. Go and get some for me'.
> Cass brings back some of the counting blocks in her classroom.
> 'OK' says the teacher 'If I ask you to get 25 blocks and share them out between five people, could you do that?'

Cass counts out 25 blocks and then, using one block at a time, counts 'one for you, one for you, one for you, one for you and one for you' five times over.
'OK' says the teacher. 'Tell me what you did'.
'I gave one to each person and then another one and then another one and then another one till they had all gone'.
'Good' says the teacher. 'You shared them out. How many did each person get?'
Cass counts each pile and says 'Five'.
'So you worked out that five goes five times into 25. Now try 27 blocks'.
Cass goes through the whole procedure again and then finds she has two left over. 'What do I do with these?' she asks.
'Good question' replies the teacher. 'What you have discovered is that five goes five times into 27 but not exactly. You have got two blocks left over.

(Personal observation)

In this example the more expert other is a teacher but it could equally well be a child. You can see how the teacher, in this example, takes seriously the child's request to learn something and through passing comments back and forth, helps the child internalise what she is learning. The teacher provides her with the language she needs to develop the concept of 'goes into' or 'division' and also allows her to begin to reflect on what she is doing as she learns. The teacher, in this reciprocal exchange, is helping the child develop *metacognitive skills* – the ability to reflect on what she has learned.

Peer teaching and reciprocal teaching are predicated on a number of things: an acceptance that all learning is social; that everyone is, at times, more expert than someone else; that children are actively seeking to understand the world; that education is not about filling up empty heads with nuggets of knowledge and that all learners – children and adults – raise questions and should be treated as equal partners in any learning situation. This is known as a *dialogic approach to learning* – learning through dialogue.

In their own words

I found this delightful extract from some work done by Susi Long with Donna Bell and Jim Brown. It is written in such an approachable voice that it immediately draws the reader into the situation being described. They were looking at young children engaged in *side-by-side reading* and this took place in a kindergarten in South Carolina. Some of the children – Juan, Martita and Marcial – were Mexican Americans and Spanish was their first language. Can you see why this has been included in this section on more expert others?

During free activity time early in the school year, Marcial walked to the bookcase and selected an English picture book. He sat on the floor and began to read the pictures (a reading strategy that had been demonstrated by the classroom teacher) aloud in Spanish. A few feet away Kiesha, an English-only kindergartner sat on the floor reading the book *Jack Be Nimble*. She used the pictures to read the story aloud in English. Kiesha finished the book, closed it and looked at Juan. He looked at her, she moved closer to him and she opened her book again, holding it so that he could see the pages. Then, Kiesha began rereading her book in English, this time reading directly to Juan. Martita moved closer so that she could also see the pages. Both Martita and Juan looked at the pictures in the book as Kiesha turned the pages and read the book aloud to them. Later, Martita and Juan sat with one another and picture-read using the same behaviours that had been demonstrated by Kiesha.

The authors' analysis was this:

In this way Kiesha subtly implemented a practice that supported Martita and Juan's participation in an English language and literacy event. As the Mexican American children watched and listened to her read, they blended their own previous experience with her demonstration of reading in English and reading with a partner to create understanding.

(Long et al., 2004, pp. 98–99)

Here no adult has suggested that a peer teaching session take place, as in Kenner's work. This arose spontaneously out of a classroom ritual and, almost certainly, a classroom culture of sharing and respect.

Implications for early years practice

As far as possible set up your room to invite and promote children learning from and teaching one another. This will almost certainly already be the case if you are working in a nursery but is less likely with older children. But if you are aware of what the children know and can do you are more likely to let them teach one another, sharing their expertise. I guess this is a request not to always turn to the child whose hand shoots up first or who is keen to show off her expertise. All the children will be expert about something. In Long's example Kiesha was clearly more expert in speaking English, and she could read the pictures just as the other children could. Speaking your first language is certainly an almost universal achievement, but learning a second language is not. Sometimes expertise is something very tiny – being able to recognise the first letter of your name, cut out using a pair of scissors, climb onto a chair or blow a soap bubble. Be alert to the small *significant moments* in the daily lives of the children – the first time you notice that the child can do something new. Record them in some way and keep them as they will show how the child is developing and learning.

See also: Apprentice, cognitive development, guided participation, peer-teaching, reciprocal teaching, scaffolding learning, Zone of Proximal Development

Annotated further reading:

Kenner, C. (2004). *Becoming biliterate: Young children learning different writing systems.* Stoke on Trent and Sterling, USA: Trentham Books.

Long, S., Bell, D. and Brown, J. (2004). In Gregory, E. (Ed.), *One child, many worlds: Early learning in multicultural communities.* London: David Fulton Publishers.

You have already found work by Kenner referred to. This second item is an extremely readable chapter in Eve Gregory's book.

Exploratory play:

Also called investigative play, where a child is trying to find answers to questions she has raised
See also key concepts: Asking questions, play, rules

Eye-pointing:

One of the ways in which infants share attention with adults. The early stages of communication and intersubjectivity
See also key concepts: Attention, intersubjectivity

Family:

The network of those closest to the child
See also key concepts: Intersubjectivity, cognitive development, decentre, documenting children's progress, ecological model, feelings, identity

Fantasy play:

Where children create and inhabit possible worlds. Also called pretend or imaginary play
See also key concepts: Asking questions, creativity, play

Feelings and their impact

Synonymous with: Emotions, affect

Words or phrases linked to this concept	What it means	Why it matters
Alienation	To be made to feel not part of a group	Being excluded is very painful emotionally
Stereotyping	An over-simplified generalisation based on no evidence and usually carrying negative implications	An individual becomes described in a very crude and offensive way based on stereotypes
Expectations	What is expected of individuals or groups	Low expectations can be damaging
Failure	Being judged to have not been as good as others	Very damaging to self-esteem
Self-esteem	Sense of oneself	Low self-esteem is very damaging

We have looked at aspects of feelings in the section on emotional development. Here I propose that we examine in more detail the feelings that give rise to children getting into trouble in settings and classes and look at some of the reasons for this. Possible causes include *stereotyping, expectations, alienation* and *failure*, all of which can impact on young children's self-esteem and hence their ability to become full participants of the culture of the class or setting. We are looking at how feelings of inferiority, anger, helplessness, difference, otherness or inadequacy can cause children to be not able to function well in groups.

We live and work in a richly diverse society and despite it having been like this for generations there are still issues that make it difficult for some children to succeed in our systems. This is a huge area and in this book there is only room to touch on the issues, but they are very important and deserve your serious thought. Let us start with stereotyping. You surely have an everyday sense of what the word means and may even have suffered from being stereotyped on the basis of perhaps being a woman, black, not an English speaker, old, young, coming from a single-parent family, or a traveller family or any one of a number of issues that set you apart from the mainstream. To be stereotyped means that certain things are attributed to you in terms of a group you 'belong' to so you, the individual, are described in ways that are almost always negative. Irish people are stereotyped as being stupid; children who speak languages other than English are stereotyped so their teachers expect them to have severe difficulties in learning; children from single-parent families are stereotyped as suffering from inadequate parenting; poor children are stereotyped as generally deprived. We all know that these are gross categorisations of groups of people based on little or no evidence and so we should disregard them. The truth is that for children, being so cruelly and crudely assessed can be extremely painful. Children who are not able to get into the group become alienated and begin to feel a lack of self-worth and this is true of children who fail.

Case study/example

First, here is Gurmit's story:

> I was seven years old when we arrived in the United Kingdom. My father came here two years before us. I could not speak or understand a word of English. I remember going to the infant school and sitting there looking around and getting frustrated. Other children used to laugh at me and bully me in the playground. I didn't know how to complain and started to respond by kicking and pushing them. After a couple of months I started to understand the playground language but still found it very hard to cope with the class-work. At the end of junior school I still could not read or spell even basic words ... Mum and Dad didn't know anything, they worked long hours and I didn't want to worry them.
>
> (Statham, 2008, p. ix)

What is your analysis of why Gurmit started behaving badly in primary school? Can you link it with being teased for being different, or being made to feel stupid or because he was just naughty?

And here are two case studies cited by Tina Hyder (2001) and arising from her work with the Refugee Playgroup in North London.

> I remember when R first started at the playgroup. He was just three and had arrived recently from Eritrea. He was so angry and frustrated he threw things around and hit other children. Over the weeks he began to trust us and start communicating with the other children. I think he really benefited from his time with us. We were a place of safety.
>
> When a four-year-old Kurdish child from Turkey arrived she also wouldn't communicate, wouldn't play, and for many weeks refused to be physically separated from her mother. It took a long time before she felt able to join in with activities and begin to work out some of her anxieties.
>
> (Hyder, 2001, p. 93)

I am sure that you understand something about how early experiences of trauma, war, having to leave your home, or witnessing hideous events will impact on children and although the two case studies here are based on events nearly 20 years ago, think of Syria today.

In her own words

Babette Brown was born in South Africa and opposed all forms of racial and other discrimination. She won the Guardian Jerwood Award in 1997 for her anti-racist work and her book *Unlearning Discrimination in the Early Years* (1998) has become a classic text. Here is a taste of her writing, which is clear, jargon-free and powerful:

> Children can become active, enthusiastic and independent learners if, as their educators, we value their culture and communities and understand how racism and other social inequalities influence their lives. With our guidance and support children can, as this example illustrates, actively challenge unfairness … The pressure under which we work can leave us feeling that we have neither the time nor the energy to confront social inequalities like racism, sexism and class discrimination. However, if anti-discriminatory practice is good practice do we in fact have a choice? Can we treat each child with equal concern if we don't appreciate the powerful effect of stereotypical thinking and behaviour on policy and practice? Can our curriculum meet the needs of each child if it is culturally inappropriate and based on discriminatory principles? Can we have discussions around racist, sexist, class or homophobic issues that arouse passionate feelings if we don't trust, respect and listen to one another?
>
> (pp. 3–4)

Implications for early years practice

Brown goes on to suggest a programme of action for those involved in the care and education of young children. The first thing to be done is to examine our own interactions with children and their parents to see if we have been subconsciously influenced by stereotypes. We might realise that we are expecting Asian girls to be quiet and submissive or West Indian boys to be loud and lively. Next we must observe children as individuals and also ourselves in how attentive we are to what is happening to the children. Do we know who is being bullied or called names or made to feel stupid? And do we just accept this or do we intervene? Do we talk to the children about the effects of their behaviour on others or operate on the basis of them being too young to understand? Then we need to look at the curriculum and see if it is genuinely allowing all the children to draw on their experience – whatever that experience might be. And we need, of course, to ensure we build a culture of listening, sharing, respecting, participating, communicating and collaborating.

See also: Attention, cognitive development, collaborate, creativity, decentre, emotional development, identity, imitation, interaction with others, meaning, play, representation and re-representation, role making and role playing

83

Annotated further reading:

Hyder, T. (2001). Supporting refugee children in the early years. In J. Rutter and C. Jones, *Refugee education: Mapping the field* (2nd ed.). Stoke on Trent: Trentham Books.
Rutter's book is useful for those involved with refugee children although some of it is rather dated.

Statham, L. (Ed.) (2008). *Counting them in: Isolated bilingual learners in schools.* Stoke on Trent and Sterling, USA: Trentham Books.
A collection of case studies about individual children who are bilingual and not with other speakers of the same languages. More useful to those working with older children.

Brown, B. (1998). *Unlearning discrimination in the early years.* Stoke on Trent: Trentham Books.
This is a wonderful book and one you should certainly read. Although it was written some time ago everything in it is relevant and important and will make you think hard about some things it is easier not to think about. It is written in straightforward language and illustrated by illuminating examples.

First-hand experience

Synonymous with: Concrete experience, direct experience, hands-on experience, everyday experiences

Words or phrases linked to this concept	What it means	Why it matters
Everyday concepts	The concepts that arise out of everyday situations in real life	This learning, where the purpose is clear to the child, does not depend on memory
Scientific concepts	More abstract concepts that do depend on memory	Needs to be preceded by development of everyday concepts
Meaningful contexts	Situations where the purpose is clear	Allows the child to draw on her own experience to make sense

Vygotsky was interested in how children move from using *everyday concepts* to being able to use *scientific concepts*. Everyday concepts, as you might imagine, are the concepts children encounter through their interactions and activities in the everyday worlds of home and community. He believed that how children acquire concepts is mediated by the cultural tool of speech. So as children live, play and interact with others they develop concepts, which are called either everyday concepts or spontaneous concepts. These might relate to ordinary life experiences such as cooking or eating or going to the clinic or sickness or the birth of a baby brother or starting school or going on holiday and so on. In other words, through their interactions, and mediated by speech, children learn the concepts relating to their lives. For Vygotsky and for others the strength of these everyday concepts is that they have arisen from direct, usually first-hand or concrete experience and have not relied on memory. First-hand experience – which means direct or practical experience – is very important and children, wherever they live, have access to such experience. Those of us involved in the care and education of young children know about this, even though we may never have used the terms 'everyday concepts' or 'spontaneous concepts'. We know about the importance of the experiences children have had before school or setting and during school and setting, but within the children's everyday lives of home and community.

Scientific concepts are those that arise through some type of instruction more often in a formal system of knowledge rather than through interactions in everyday life. The child, in a formal educational setting, is exposed to some of the abstract conceptual knowledge of their culture. A child in a school in Kenya, for example, may be learning about some abstract concepts in common with a child in Sussex (dark and light, perhaps or long and short), but also some very different concepts (uses of cow dung as fuel, for example). Through interactions with a more knowledgeable person, adult or child, the learner is introduced to these more abstract and more general concepts.

Margaret Donaldson says that where young children can deal first with the concrete – by which she means something set in a meaningful context where the purpose is evident to the learner – she will be better able to deal with abstract issues and concepts that are dependent on memory and hence on prior first-hand experience.

Case study/example

> In our experiments, a child who rarely spoke learned the meanings of five words (i.e. chair, table, cabinet, couch, bookcase) with no particular difficulty. He clearly would have been able to extend the series. However, he could not learn the word 'furniture'. Though the child could easily learn any word from the series of subordinate concepts, this more general word was impossible for him. Learning the word 'furniture' represented something more than the addition of a sixth word to the five that the child had already mastered. It represented the mastery of the relationship of generality. The mastery of the word 'furniture' represented the mastery of the child's first higher order concept, a concept that would include a series of more specific subordinate concepts.
>
> (Vygotsky, 1987, p. 225, cited in Smidt, 2009)

This extract serves a double purpose. It tells you something about abstraction (a higher order process) and its difficulties for young learners, but it also gives you an idea of Vygotsky's voice. Do you understand what he is saying? The case study does not refer directly to first-hand experience but implies that being able to understand and use words for items like chair and table reflect the first-hand experience the child might have had with everyday objects. You can see and touch a chair. You can sit on it. But what is furniture? It is not something you can see or touch, taste or smell. It is a category made up of items that have some feature in common – or a generality in Vygotsky's terms.

 ## Implications for early years practice

Very obvious, really, to ensure that the experiences and areas you offer and set up allow children to move from the concrete to the abstract. So you need to ensure that they have objects to manipulate and experiences where the purpose is clear.

 See also: Cognitive development, decentre, interaction with others

 ## Annotated further reading:

Donaldson, M. (1987). *Children's minds*. London: Fontana.

Already recommended, this book is easy to read and certainly worth doing so.

Formats

Synonymous with: Routines of the day

Word or phrase linked to this concept	What it means	Why it matters
Cyclical repetitions	Repeated over and over again	Allows the child to expect and predict
Cyclical time	Time that moves in cycles	Allows the child to expect and predict
Request mode	Learning to ask for something	All referring to children's growing competence and sophistication as a language user
Pretend mode	Learning to behave as if	
Prelinguistic	Before language, usually referring to spoken language	

In the lives of all infants there are certain things that need to be done to ensure that the infant is clean, dry, fed, rested and healthy. These *cyclical repetitions* of daily events with some changes and variations are what we are calling the daily routines. They can take place in the home of the baby or in a setting and they seem to represent a significant step in the life of the child, allowing the child to form and maintain relationships with adults (parents or carers) and peers. Bruner called these routines *formats* and said that they are what allow infants to come to understand cyclical time. It seems that the child pays attention to the repeated gestures and actions and sounds that take place during the repeated rituals and this enables the child to recognise and then anticipate and predict what has happened and might happen. Through interaction with an adult or a more experienced other in the format the infant becomes able to influence and regulate it. During the changing of a nappy, for example, there is a fixed routine but this is accompanied by variation in terms of who changes the baby, what that person says or does, when it happens, and so on.

Bruner believed that, for the child to be able to generate the rules of grammar, there has to have been a history of social and conceptual experience. He said that this experience must have taken place within routinised and familiar formats. It is these very routines that make up his Language Acquisition Support System, which you can read about under Language acquisition.

Case study/example

Bruner (1983) suggested four ways that his Language Acquisition Support System can help the child move from prelinguistic to linguistic communication:

1. Within the familiar and routinised formats adults become able to highlight those features of the world that are known and important to the child and that have a basic and simple grammatical form. So a format is a predictable routine repetition of language.
    *   Lifting the child from sleep saying 'upsadaisy' or some other word or phrase routinely used to accompany this action.
    *   Saying 'Wave bye-bye to daddy/mummy' (or the equivalent in whatever is the child's first language) and waving whilst saying it.
    *   Saying something like 'Here comes the train' as the spoonful of food approaches the baby's mouth.
2. The adult helps the child by encouraging and modelling lexical and phrasal substitutes for familiar gestural and vocal means. This is what enables the child to learn to ask for something and master the use of what Bruner calls the request mode.
    *   The baby points to the banana on the table and makes a sound and the adult says 'Oh, so you want a banana do you?'
    *   The baby shakes her arms up and down in frustration and the adult says 'What do you want?'

3. Where the child has chosen what to do in play the child may operate in the *pretend mode*, which is a rich field for language learning and language use. The language children use in pretend play as they try out different roles is fascinating, as they mimic the tones of voice, the inflections and intonations and the grammar and vocabulary of whoever it is they are 'being'.

> Four-year-old Barney, involved in role play, explores death and destruction. Here is what he says 'Help, help! … I'm destroying! The king! The invisible bad king! He told me to get you. If I don't he'll put glue all over me. I'm turning into a statue! Now I'm all chained up. I'm in glue prison'.
>
> (Paley, 1988, p. 118)

This is extraordinary use of language very unlikely to be heard in anything other than fantasy play.

4. When the primary caregiver and the child have had much experience of routinised formats they are able to generalise from one format to another. So they will jointly engage in activities that help the child use things like request (asking for something), the interrogative (ask questions), reference (talking about something) and so on.

In his own words

For Bruner, formats were intimately related to scaffolding or supporting learning. The formats provided a linguistic version of scaffolding within a routine/everyday and repeated task. Here the primary caregiver and the child share an intention to get something done with words. Before the child is able to do this the carer does it for her but as soon as the child becomes able the carer expects the child to contribute. One of the formats that Bruner and his colleagues studied was reading. In the situation described the caregiver is with the child looking at a picture book, with the adult reading the story or talking about the pictures and implicitly inviting the child to join in. Initially this book sharing provides an opportunity for the child to reference or name. Reading proved a very stable routine.

> Each step of the way, the mother incorporated whatever competences the child had already developed – to be clued by pointing, to appreciate that sounds 'stood for' things and events, etc. The mother remained the constant throughout. Thereby she was his scaffold – calling his attention, making a query, providing an answering label if he lacked one, and confirming his offer of one, whatever it might be. As he gained competence she would raise her criterion. Almost any vocalisation the child

might offer at the start would be accepted. But each time the child came close to the standard form, she would hold out for it. What was changing was, of course, what the mother *expected* in response – and that, of course, was 'fine-tuned' by her 'theory' of the child's capacities.

(Bruner, 1983, pp. 171–172)

Implications for early years practice

For those of you working with babies and toddlers, you will know that the routines of the day take up much of the time. It is a reminder to you to use these repeated routines as opportunities to interact with the children and use spoken language as well as little games and songs involving repetition and prediction. In other words, use formats.

 See also: Attention, narrative

Annotated further reading:

Addessi, A. R. (2009). The musical dimension of daily routines with under-four children during diaper change, bedtime and free-play. *Early Child Development and Care, 179*(6), 747–768. Available at: http://dx.doi.org/10.1080/03004430902944122

If you can download Addessi's fascinating paper it is worth reading. She describes an action-research project being undertaken by the University of Bologna, looking at how routines of the day enable children to explore aspects of music as one of the possible communication systems available to them.

Gender:

In relation to equality of access and opportunity

See also key concepts: Agency, complex environments, Developmentally Appropriate Practice, ecological model

Guided participation

Synonymous with: Apprentice, learning through participation, modelling and imitation

Words or phrases linked to this concept	What it means	Why it matters
Active participants	Children who take part in events alongside others	Interaction, modelling, imitation and more
Individual plane	Some development takes place within the child	Some learning can take place alone
Social plane	With another person	Some learning takes place through interaction with one or more people
Sociocultural plane or context	With other people in a meaningful context	Most learning takes place with others doing things that make sense to the learners – like cooking, making things, planting – the events of everyday life
Intersubjectivity	The shared meaning that arises from interactions	An interaction that includes both parties knowing what the others are focused on
Scaffolding	The more expert other helps the learner take small steps of learning	Helps child move from dependence to independence in cognitive activities
Dyadic interaction	A dyad means a pair so this is an interaction between two people	
Human sense	Where the purpose is clear to the learners	Essential ingredient in early learning

Barbara Rogoff worked in the United States and with communities in developing countries, particularly in Latin America, where she noted how children were more involved in the real life of families and community. This meant that they were *active participants* in the processes, routines and rituals of adult daily life. She watched as children were inducted into the particular practices of families and communities through what she called *guided participation*. This guided participation was sometimes through being alongside an experienced person, or more expert other, watching what they were doing, sometimes through social interaction such as talking about what was being done and sometimes through direct teaching. Her view of development involves three interacting planes on which development occurs. These are the *individual plane* within the child herself; the *social plane*, involving other people within the community within which the child lives and the actual *sociocultural context* that defines the manner in which these people engage in the processes of making and sharing meaning.

Can you see how this view allows her to analyse the learning she sees taking place in terms of the time and place, the culture and the context?

Case study/example

The example cited earlier in this book to illustrate children asking questions is here used as an example of guided participation in action.

> Three children are alongside their mother who is making tortillas on the fire. She gives them each a lump of dough and they watch what she is doing and imitate her, throwing the dough, flattening it and rolling it. They watch not only their mother but also one another. Here they are doing and memorising individually as they are involved with other people within the cultural context of making the bread of their community.
>
> (Adapted from the work of Rogoff)

In their own words

Since you have encountered Rogoff's words in other contexts I am offering you here an extract from an article about Rogoff's work. The authors are Maureen Vandermaas-Peeler, Erin Way and Jennifer Umpleby (2002).

> Rogoff (1990) described guided participation as a collaborative process in which children participate in on-going routines and activities guided by other, more competent, members of the culture. Through intersubjectivity, or a shared focus of attention, both the child and the adult or other 'expert' have a shared interest and sense of purpose in the task at hand (Rogoff, 1990). In order to help the child develop more advanced skills and to reach an eventual goal of independence, parents and others provide guidance and support to encourage and ensure the child's skill development. Providing appropriate levels of intervention or support so that the child gradually increases his or her competencies has been termed *scaffolding* (Wood et al., 1976). Support or scaffolding should be provided at a level that is challenging to the child but not overly frustrating. This is consistent with Vygotsky's (1978) concept of the zone of proximal development, or the difference between what a child can do alone and in collaboration with a more skilled partner. Thus, children learn through their social interactions with more competent members of the culture, who provide guidance in various culturally relevant activities.
>
> Cross-cultural research has demonstrated the importance of considering adult–child relationships within the relevant sociocultural context. For example, research on children's play has demonstrated that in many cultures, such as in Guatemalan

(Goncu and Mosier, 1991), Mayan (Gaskins, 1996; Rogoff, 1981), and Mexican (Farver, 1993) communities, adults do not engage in play with children because they do not believe themselves to be appropriate play partners. In these cultures, it is often the older siblings who scaffold children's play. The context for the dyadic interaction in the present study, baking cookies, differs from many Western studies of adult guidance of children's development, in that it represents an adult-oriented activity rather than a child-oriented task such as playing. Although there are cultural variations in the degree to which children participate in adult routines (Rogoff, 1981), children around the world typically become involved to some extent in the on-going adult activities around them. From an early age, children may be asked to help in small ways with household work.

(Vandermaas-Peeler et al., 2002, p. 548)

This is important because it means that we cannot see development itself as a universal term. Rather, it must involve the acquisition of those skills and knowledge practices that are important to the community involved rather than to a generalised community. Rogoff had a profound influence on those thinking about children as being essentially rooted in a culture, a context, a group and a time. This means that many studies of children learning and developing across the world look at children in the groups in which they operate. These include people looking at mixed groups of language speakers (like Eve Gregory, Charmian Kenner and others); those looking at how children learn, adapt and make culture in groups (like Marsh, Siraj-Blatchford, Kress) and researchers in Africa who insist on the primacy of taking account of culture and context in all things (like Nsamenang, Biersteker).

Rogoff paid particular attention to what children do when they are involved in the everyday real-life activities of homes and communities. She paid attention to what the younger children were doing as they were alongside more expert others and that led her to think about interaction, using others as models of how to become experts, and the roles of learner and teacher.

Implications for early years practice

Rogoff's work in general is a reminder of the importance of taking account of the context in which the children are learning. She reminds us that children learn wherever they are and do so alongside and from their peers as well as adults. By looking at the children in their homes and communities she is inevitably looking at learning situations that make human sense to the children. They can see the purpose of the activities. This is a reminder to us to offer such opportunities for young children whenever we can.

She also reminds us that children learn not only at school or in a setting, but everywhere. She invites us to remember that the learning that takes place away from our eyes and ears must be as valued and respected as the learning we observe or partake in.

See also: Apprentice, collaboration, culture, interaction with others, intersubjectivity, meaningful contexts, play

 Annotated further reading:

Rogoff, B. (1990). *Apprenticeship in thinking: Cognitive development in social context.* Oxford: Oxford University Press.

Rogoff, B. (2003). *The cultural nature of development.* Oxford: Oxford University Press.

Vandermaas-Peeler, M., Way, E. and Umpleby, J. (2002). Guided participation in a cooking activity over time. *Early Child Development and Care, 172*(6), 547–554, DOI: 10.1080/03004430215104. Available at: http://dx.doi.org/10.1080/03004430215104

The Vandermaas-Peeler et al. article is an interesting and clearly written account of a small-scale research project and you might like to download the journal article to read in full. I think it offers a good example of how to make academic writing readable but not patronising.

Habitus:

Bourdieu's word to describe a system of disposition, habits or attitudes that account for the differences evident in all societies
See also key concepts: Agency, culture

Higher Order Cognitive Processes:

The features of abstract thinking and problem solving
See also key concepts: Asking questions, attention, bilingualism, collaboration, culture, expert others, first-hand experience, meaning

Human sense:

Situations where the purpose of the activity is evident to the learners
See also key concepts: Apprentice, complex environments, decentre, guided participation

Hundred Languages of Children:

Malaguzzi's term for the expressive arts – all the ways in which we can communicate thoughts and feelings
See also key concepts: Creativity, DAP, documenting children's progress

Identity

Synonymous with: Self-image, self-concept, who you are

Words and phrases linked to this concept	What it means	Why it matters
Polycropping	Based on the shared and social rather than individual and unique	Indicates diversity of ways of constructing identity

The word identity is a common-sense word whose meaning will be clear to you and so you may be surprised at how many learned articles, couched in the most dense of academic languages, have been written on the subject. One of the things the human infant does as she journeys from dependence to independence is become aware of who she is. And who she is will vary according to when and where she is, who she is with and what they are doing. I am sure that when you think of your own identity it will change according to those factors. And you will not be surprised to know that how you define yourself will be influenced by how you believe that others define you.

So how does the human infant accomplish the extremely complex task of coming to know who she is? She begins to define her identity by starting to see herself as unique but also as connected to others. For most infants these others are members of the immediate family and, for some, the more extended family and then, perhaps the local community and neighbourhood. Here the child begins to interact with people and in doing this learns to see others as having feelings and intentions. Young children begin to pay attention to what others say and do: in part they mimic what they see and hear and they also internalise ways of acting, speaking and being. These build into a store of memories that can be drawn on in the complex scripts they will develop to play out the roles they need to play. It is in their role play that we begin to actually see them constructing their own identity.

Children construct their identities from their experiences and through their interactions. This includes seeing themselves as part of a group sharing a culture. The ways in which they and other members of their group are represented will be crucial in doing this. So children construct their identities partially from how they (the group) are represented. It will feel very different being the only black child in an all-white class, or being the only girl on the football team, for example. How children define and identify themselves is a complex process and one that essentially involves their self-esteem. The reactions of others to them or to their group impact on self-image and hence on self-identity. Children who encounter few or predominantly negative images of themselves and their group will suffer damage to their self-esteem and the whole process of identity construction will be difficult.

Developing a cultural identity is a fundamental and complex task for all young children and takes place initially within the family and then broadens out into the wider community and society. Children acquire a sense of 'belonging' to their own culture, which allows them to accept and coexist with individuals of other beliefs and cultures. The experiences children have will vary according to the values and traditions and customs and beliefs of their individual families, and the culture of the family will shape identity in unique ways.

Case study/examples: In their own words

The image of identity development in African cultures is that of 'polycropping', not monoculture; in other words, it emphasises the shared and social, rather than the unique and individual, aspects of identity. ... Traditional African cultures transcend Vygotsky's sociocultural view of identity construction by encouraging children from an early age to seek out others, particularly their peers, in order to 'gain significance from and through their relationships with others'.

(Pence & Nsamenang, 2008, p. 40)

Implications for early years practice

Encourage role play. It allows children to try on different roles to feel what it is like to be powerful or powerless, strong or weak, lonely, secure, afraid, excited and much more. Also do remember that children's construction of identity carries on for a long time – way beyond your setting – and be sensitive to what it is the child is seeking to discover about herself.

See also: Agency, attention, bilingualism, cognitive development, ecological model, feelings, interaction with others, relationships, role making and playing.

Annotated further reading:

Pence, A. and Nsamenang. B. (2008). A case for early childhood development in sub-Saharan Africa. *Working Papers in Early Childhood Development*. Bernard van Leer Foundation.

This gives you a non-Western view of identity construction. Available at: http://www.bernardvanleer.org/a_case_for_early_childhood_development_in_sub-saharan_africa

Imitation

Synonymous with: Copying, mimicry

Words or phrases linked to this concept	What it means	Why it matters
Theory of mind	Understand that others have thoughts	Significant step in learning about other human beings
Mirror neurons	A mirror neuron is a neuron that fires when a person acts or when they observe the same action. So it mirrors the behaviour of others as though the observer were himself acting	Much debated but it is clear that being able to both copy and initiate an action is significant to learning
Kinaesthesia	Your internal feelings about your body	

You all understand what imitation means and have probably not thought hard about its significance in learning. I used to think it was something children did for a while and that it did not play a very significant role in learning. But it seems that imitation is not only important in learning but is governed by what are known as *mirror neurons*, which may be important for understanding the actions of other people as well as for learning new skills by imitation. Some researchers also speculate that mirror neurons may simulate observed actions, and thus contribute to *theory of mind* skills, while others relate mirror neurons to language abilities.

Time to meet three new theorists: Alison Gopnik, Andrew Meltzoff and Patricia Kuhl. Meltzoff, in particular, developed an interest in imitation and mirror neurons, and together they co-authored a book called *The Scientist in the Crib*. Here is what they say about imitation. You may have read about or even seen the now famous experiment where an adult sticks out his tongue at a newborn baby and the baby imitates this. Think about it. Does it seem just strange or something really quite remarkable?

In their own words

At first glance this ability to imitate might seem curious and cute, but not deeply significant. But if you think about it a minute it is actually amazing. There are no mirrors in the womb: newborns have never seen their own face. So how could they know whether their tongue is inside or outside their mouth? There is another way of knowing what your face is like. As you read this, you probably have a good idea of your facial expression (we hope intense concentration leavened by the occasional smile.) Try sticking out your tongue (in a suitably private setting). The way you know you've succeeded is through kinaesthesia […] In order to imitate, newborn babies must somehow understand the similarity between that internal feeling and the external face they see, a round shape with a long pink thing at the bottom moving back and forth. Newborn babies not only distinguish and prefer faces, they also seem to recognise that those faces are like their own face. They recognise that other people are 'like me.'

(Gopnik et al., 2001, p. 30)

You will almost certainly recognise what an approachable writing style they have and perhaps you will be tempted to read their books. I enjoy them but find some of the tone a little too jokey and sometimes sentimental.

Do you know that there are some theorists who believed that children acquire their first language(s) purely through imitation? Babies certainly imitate: it is part of all learning but there is more to it than that.

In their own words again

[B]abies aren't just able to imitate us, they are driven to do so. Babies love to copy adult sounds. Pat and Andy found that when five-month-olds listen to a simple vowel like ee for fifteen minutes in the laboratory, they will coo back with a vowel of their own that resembles the one they heard. They can't make perfect ees, but they already have an idea of what to do with their mouths to make a sound that resembles ee. They have learned that ee is produced when people raise their tongue and retract their lips. Just hearing a grown-up produce the sound motivates babies to try to produce it themselves.

(Gopnik et al., 2001, pp. 124–125)

Oh clever babies!

A case study to delight you

Yo-Ann was videotaped at weekly intervals between the ages of 3 and 16 months in an attempt to capture the emergence of the ability to mimic, and to learn something of its antecedents. At each session, Yo and her mother spent 10 minutes in natural interaction that at later ages included concentrated attempts to elicit mimicry of the mother's actions.

In the first few sessions Yo-Ann's mother did not know what the purpose of the study was but knew that the researcher was interested in infant imitation. She spontaneously and unconsciously imitated her baby despite deliberate attempts not to do so. In later sessions, she collaborated in the attempt to elicit behavioural matching from her daughter.

Just before her first birthday the baby began to reproduce certain of the mother's behaviours. All were behaviours that Yo herself had spontaneously and repeatedly produced at home and that her parents had repeatedly imitated. For example, when Yo raised both arms, her parents imitated the action and said 'Bonsai!' In the weeks that followed sequences of imitation were recorded and the sequence was like this: the mother imitated something the baby did, invariably with an accompanying sound. After many such pairings, the baby reproduced the action on cue with the cue being either the action with the sound, or the sound alone, but never just the action alone. The strong impression was that the baby was producing the action either in order to reproduce the sound, or in response to a sound cue, but not as an action match to the sight of the mother's behaviour. For example, at 10 months, Yo responded to her mother's production of 'lalala' sounds, made with a wide open mouth and exaggerated tongue movements, with wide-mouthed 'la-la-la' sounds of her own. However, when Yo's mother made exaggerated tongue movements without the sounds, Yo did not respond. It seemed clear that Yo did not know what action she herself was doing when she made the 'la-la' sounds, and so did not recognize the tongue movements that her mother made and could not reproduce them. Instead, she reproduced the sounds and it just so happened that she moved her tongue to do so. It seemed clear that if Yo had been able to find her tongue at birth, she had lost that ability by 10 months of age.

(Jones, 2006, pp. 2–3)

Implications for early years practice

It is important to recognise that children will imitate one another, and you, the teacher. You may be surprised to hear just your tone of voice when children are role playing being the teacher. If you are working with babies it would be interesting to document examples of them imitating and share these with parents, telling them how this is all part of learning and development.

See also: Cognitive development, creativity, emotional development, feelings, guided participation, interaction with others, meaning, representation and re-representation

Annotated further reading

Gopnik, A., Meltzoff, A. and Kuhl, P. (2001). *The scientist in the crib: What early learning tells us about the mind*. New York. Harper Perennial.

This is an easy to read and interesting book and the authors are highly regarded in many circles. It would make a useful addition to your library, if you have started to build one.

In pretend mode:

Playing as if
See also key concepts: Formats, identity, play

Inclusion/diversity

Synonymous with: Equal opportunities, equality of access, multilingualism and multi-culturalism

(There is no table of terms at the beginning of this concept because writers seem able to write about it with little jargon.)

Some 20 years ago, *The Salamanca Statement: Framework for Action for Special Needs Education* (Unesco, 1994) was drawn up by representatives from 92 governments and 25 international organisations. It called for inclusion to be the norm and a related conference adopted a 'Framework for Action' that would require all children to be accommodated in mainstream schools, regardless of their physical, intellectual, social, emotional and linguistic abilities or other needs. It also stated that national and local policies should require that disabled children attend the neighbourhood school that the child would have attended had she not had a disability. The Statement insisted on the provision of education for all 'within the regular system' and the Centre for Studies in Inclusive Education (CSIE) regarded such inclusive schooling as the best way to address discrimination in its various forms:

> Regular schools with this inclusive orientation are the most effective means of combating discriminatory attitudes, creating welcoming communities, building

on an inclusive society and achieving education for all; moreover, they provide an effective education to the majority of children and improve the efficiency and ultimately the cost-effectiveness of the entire education system.

(CSIE, 1995, p. 8. Available at: https://www.european-agency.org/ sites/default/files/salamanca-statement-and-framework.pdf)

All of this is underpinned by economic as well as sociological, political and educational goals. But there are those who argue that there is the danger of children being physically included but excluded in terms of access to the curriculum and emotionally excluded because of alienation or isolation from peers. There is no mention of the need for properly trained teachers, essential if inclusion is to be successful. Cathy Nutbrown (1998) said that early education at its best is inclusive education – perhaps because of its emphasis on individual needs, developmentally appropriate practice and intrinsic involvement of parents. Some would cite Reggio Emilia as a model for inclusive education.

In her own words

Nurse (2001) said:

> My impression of Reggio Emilia's response to children with special needs is that the preschools minimise the effects of disability and a slower rate of learning because the learning environment matches the developmental and social needs of the individual child. ... A difference between the system in the UK and the Reggio response is the commitment to children learning as a group, from each other ... Reggio Emilia is a stable, prosperous and cohesive community. The preschools are a highly regarded part of that community which in turn values the group experience they offer to young children. Provision is local so the children are not placed in distant centres which isolate them and their families from their own community.
>
> (p. 68)

It is important to remember that inclusion speaks not only of children with disabilities but others who are treated as 'special' for a range of reasons. There are children with behavioural difficulties; children who are refugees; children who speak languages other than English. How will you set up your provision to meet such a wide range of needs?

Implications for early years practice

Ang, in her excellent article on diversity, gives us all much to think about in terms of practice by saying that practitioners need to be empowered to understand and challenge the complex issues involved for those in the early years. She says:

The aim of initial teacher training and professional development programmes, for instance, is to enable practitioners to deal with issues of diversity in their own setting with confidence and autonomy. Practitioners have to be critically aware of their own cultural framework, and the ways in which their behaviour, caregiving routines and curriculum plans are determined by their own cultural, familial and individual values. The basis of an effective curriculum is for practitioners to have a critical understanding of these influences and differences in order that they may be able to make adjustments in their own practices and provisions, and provide care and education for children in culturally appropriate ways. It is therefore important for early years professionals to discuss potential conflict situations, to learn to dialogue about what they believe to be good practice, and to be open to other cultural perspectives even those that may conflict with their own. Practitioners and educators who themselves come from a dominant culture and speak only a dominant language must become critical of the effects of their own cultural and linguistic positioning. Do we, for instance, accept that there are different varieties of English?

(Ang, 2010, p. 50)

The excerpt above serves as a reminder that advocating social justice and, indeed, valuing cultural diversity, is about critiquing the normalising discourses through the curriculum and the pedagogies that we employ. It is also, I would argue, about creating inclusive, hybrid curricular spaces for both practitioners and children.

 See also: Bilingualism, complex environments, culture, identity, mark-making

 Annotated further reading:

Ang, L. (2010). Critical perspectives on cultural diversity in early childhood: Building an inclusive curriculum and provision. *Early Years: An International Research Journal,* *30*(1), 50.
This is an excellent, thoughtful and thought-provoking article on a serious issue and one very relevant to us all. Do try to read it.

Nutbrown, C. and Clough, P. (2004). Inclusion and exclusion in the early years: Conversations with European educators. *European Journal of Special Needs Education,* *19*(3).
Interesting but possibly difficult to access.

Inner speech:

When external speech is internalised it becomes inner speech, which is really synonymous with thought

See also key concepts: Asking questions, cognitive development, egocentric, language, monologues

Interaction with others

Synonymous with: Communication, synergy, intercommunication, reciprocal action, cooperation

Words or phrases linked to this concept	What it means	Why it matters
Knowledge-making tools	Another word for cultural tools	Vital for creating and sharing meaning
Sociohistorical context	In light of history and social change	One way of looking at things that is firmly rooted in culture
Beliefs and practices	Religions, ideas and customs within groups	The things that make up one of many ways of living
Ownership	When something belongs to you	In order to understand the learner must make what she is learning her own
Internalising	When it is possible to consider something in the absence of the real object or event	An essential feature of being a successful learner, which enables you to think abstractly
Mental images/ mental maps	A memory of something already experienced and 'stored' in the brain	Something remembered can be accessed again and again and does not depend on the concrete

Vygotsky said that all knowledge and all the *knowledge-making tools* (which are cultural tools like books, pens, communication systems) available to a community must be considered within a *sociohistorical context*. Your community and mine each has a set of *beliefs and practices* that govern the way in which the world operates and that have been developed over generations and collectively represent its history. My community includes being an immigrant, being a non-believer, valuing reading and music and education, enjoying Middle Eastern food, speaking English and some other languages, enjoying families and so on. And although I have lived in the UK for more than half my life I am still not a full participant in some very English things – country fairs, the world of Gilbert and Sullivan, the customs of Eton and more. Your community will probably share some but not all of these beliefs and ways of operating. The ways in which the beliefs and customs are passed down from generation to generation are through the language and the symbols used to communicate these whilst they are being made part of the culture through participation. I sat alongside my grandfather whilst he chanted Yiddish rhymes. You may have worked alongside your mother making pasta or alongside your siblings at Sunday School or watching your mother dress in her burkha. The child takes ownership of knowledge through *internalising* first on the social level of interacting with others and subsequently by making the action her own. We learn first through being alongside more experienced others and then we internalise or make *mental images or maps* of what has been experienced and understood. In light of this we can say that the acquisition of knowledge and the making of meaning may best be viewed as being socially and culturally determined rather than individually constructed. We are moving away from the lone rational scientist to the collaborative learner. This is an important idea and it is worth reading it again.

Case study/example

Here is an example of four-year-old children at play, recreating and sharing their culture. It comes again from the wonderful work of Vivian Gussin Paley. This group of children are obsessed with bad guys. And there are firm rules relating to these bad guys, all of which have been developed by the children. A bad guy cannot have a birthday or a name or share in any play sequence with a baby. And once he has been spotted he has to be dealt with quickly.

'Keep makin' gold' Barney orders. 'You're the walkout guards and the goldmakers. Don't forget. I'm the guard that controls the guns.'
'But we control the guns when you sleep,' Frederick decides.
'No. You make the gold and I control the guns. Anyway, I'm not sleeping because there's bad guys coming. Calling all guards! Stuart, get on. You wanna be a guard? Bad guys! They see the ship because it's already the sun.'
'No bad guys, Barney' Mollie cautions. 'The baby is sleeping.'
'There hasta be bad guys, Mollie. We gots the cannons.'
'You can't shoot when the baby is sleeping.'

(Paley, 1988, p. 19)

How hard these children are working in this world they have created. They need to develop some rules to hold the narrative together and they do this largely on the basis of what they have learned through stories read and told, real events in their lives, and values and beliefs of their homes and societies.

Rogoff believed that internalisation actually takes place on three planes rather than two and this third plane is that of the binding context of where the learning takes place – the sociocultural context.

In his own words

Trevarthen has focused on the sociocultural aspects of learning in the human infant and on how important others and communication and sharing of ideas are to all learning. His views are expressed in an amazing article (2011). This is a very abbreviated part of this article, which is really worth reading.

> The natural creativity and cooperation of infants and toddlers, their self-produced motives for acting and knowing with other people, are given less attention than their needs for care and protection. ... Infants under one year, who have no language, communicate much more powerfully and constructively with receptive adults than psychological science of rational processes has expected (Trevarthen 2008). They engage their interests and emotions with the purposes and feelings of other persons from birth, and they rapidly develop skilful capacities for regulating intimate encounters with humour, teasing, and moral evaluations of different persons. ... More important than the fact that these abilities and sensibilities are attained so early is the finding of detailed and unprejudiced observational research that there is a self- directed programme of development – a natural sequence of age-related stages in the growth of the child's body and brain, and in consciousness and activity, especially in communication (Trevarthen and Aitken 2003). The child's motives for engaging in play with other persons are the core of a specific human adaptation for the collaborative creation of meaning or 'cultural learning' (Trevarthen 2001; Frank and Trevarthen 2010). This making common sense in responsive companionship is growing in every child from prenatal stages. It is strong, and can be recruited by a consciously receptive and supportive human environment to improve the abilities and awareness of a child with severe disabilities, or one who has earlier suffered abusive, neglectful or unresponsive parenting and is emotionally damaged (Hughes 2006; Juffer, Bakermans- Kranenburg, and van Ijzendoorn 2008).
>
> (pp. 175–176)

I love the term responsive companionship used for what I have been calling interaction.

🎎 *Implications for early years practice*

Set up your provision to be as collaborative in its approach as possible. Take notice of the relationships children make and make notes on how they communicate with one another. Do not ever underestimate a child on the basis of age. Have high expectations for all children in terms of being part of social groups and communicating verbally and in other ways in order to make and share meanings.

See also: Active learner, agency, attention, cognitive development, collaboration, DAP, documenting progress, expert others, feelings, first-hand experience, guided participation, identity, imitation

Annotated further reading:

Trevarthen, C. (2011). What young children give to their learning, making education work to sustain a community and its culture. *European Early Childhood Education Research Journal*, *19*(2), 173–193. DOI: 10.1080/1350293X.2011.574405. Available at: http://dx.doi.org/10.1080/1350293X.2011.574405

Intersubjectivity

Synonymous with: Shared attention/understanding/sustained shared attention

Words or phrases linked to the concept	What it means	Why it matters
Secondary intersubjectivity	After sharing attention, the child with another is able to have an exchange focused largely around objects	Becoming aware that others have ideas and needs and feelings
Tertiary intersubjectivity	In an exchange with others the child is able to have an exchange more focused on issues like ownership	A clear indication that the child is able to read the minds and feelings of others
Dyadic	Between two individuals	
Triadic	Between three individuals	
Social referencing	The ability to work out what people feel through their non-verbal communication	Children begin to be able to interpret what expressions and gestures mean
Meta-representation	The ability to pretend and to understand pretence in others	Has ethical consequences
Proto-conversation	Communication without words	Essential to being human, this is the start of sharing ideas

Intersubjectivity is an interaction between two conscious minds and is something that has interested researchers and theorists in early childhood. We know that the human infant is interested in and responsive to the emotions and the behaviour of others. The work of Colwyn Trevarthen (1977), cited in the concept of attention earlier in this book in the issue of attention, is repeated here as an example of intersubjectivity where attention is a key issue. It has been shown that infants as young as two months of age show a different response to someone who speaks to them than to someone else in the room who remains silent. It seems that human development is almost naturally social, in the sense that humans are inclined to react socially in cultural contexts and to both make and share meaning. Those who adopt this view of development see relationships and communications with others as the most significant feature of the child's environment.

Trevarthen, as long ago as 1995, went further and looked at how children come to learn the very culture into which they have been born. He asked why it is that very young children are so keen to learn the language and all the other habits, customs, rituals and beliefs of the community around them. He said that a three-year-old child is a socially aware person who can make and keep friends and negotiate and cooperate with many different people in many different situations. Young children primarily make sense of the world through interactions with others, by sharing. They use their emotions and the emotions of others that they have intuited to categorise experiences that will help them cooperate. For many years Trevarthen has been analysing, in minute detail, videos of infants and their mothers and in doing this he has been made aware of some things that made him turn to a concept first introduced by the philosopher, Habermas. This is *intersubjectivity* and a common-sense definition of intersubjectivity is having a shared understanding. Both partners must come to a shared understanding of both the issue (or the event) and the intention (or the purpose).

When children are about nine months old, Tomasello (1997) noted that the mother will follow the child's gaze to determine what the child is interested in or paying attention to (or vice versa with the child following the mother's gaze or actions). Attention becomes shared around what is being focused on and it is this shared focus of attention that now moves beyond the here-and-now interaction into the world of objects – perhaps toys, or food or other people. This is a really important point.

Case study/example

> Uri looks at his mother and sees her looking out of the window. He sees the car out of the window and points to it. 'Yes', says the mother, interpreting the question he cannot yet ask through following the child's gaze. 'Your daddy's home'.

Trevarthen called this *secondary intersubjectivity* and believed that its importance was that it allowed the infant to develop a realisation that the events, objects and people in the world and the actions made on or with these, can be experienced by more than one person. This means that the child is ready to share meanings with peers and it is through their new symbolic competence that children can construct and develop intersubjectivity in peer interactions. This involves them in discussion, negotiation, sharing meaning and collaborating. Various writers talk also of tertiary intersubjectivity where the exchange between the participants' focuses on the value of things rather than the things themselves. This is indicated in the table below:

Type	Context	What behaviours are involved	Process	From
Mirroring	Face-to-face exchange	Imitation	Related to mirror neurons and a seeming instinctive urge to copy	Birth
Primary intersubjectivity	Dyadic exchanges – between two partners	Protoconversations and social expectations	Emotional co-regulation – responding to one another	2 months
Secondary intersubjectivity	Triadic exchanges – between three people and about objects	Involves joint attention and social referencing	Intentional communication and intentional co-experience	9 months
Tertiary intersubjectivity	Triadic exchanges about the value of things	Embarrassment, self-recognition, claims of ownership, use of possessives, pro-social behaviours	Projection and ability to recognise aspects of self in others	20 months
Ethical stance	Decisions about the value of things in terms of justice, equity and so on	Claim of ownership, sharing, distributive justice, theories of mind	Value negotiation with others, narration, meta-representation of reputation	4 years

Source: Adapted from Rochat et al. (2009)

This looks terrifying but in reality it makes perfect sense. The human infant moves from knowing herself to knowing others. At first the child, in face-to-face encounters with another, watches and mirrors or imitates what she sees. This is *mirroring* in the first row of the table. From about two months old the human infant, in an exchange with another, is able to *share meaning through communicating with sounds or eye-pointing*. The child looks repeatedly at a biscuit and back at the mother. From about nine months the child with others is able to *communicate about objects*. This involves the children in *joint attention* and *social referencing*, which means the ability to 'read' the body language of others. From 20 months children are able to communicate with others about things other than objects; things like whose toy is it, or claiming to be right, and more. When children are about four years old they can go beyond just holding tight to a toy to arguing logically for their entitlement to have it.

In their own words

Our intention was to revise the development of intersubjectivity, stressing that it originates from reciprocal social exchanges that include imitation, empathy, but also negotiation from which meanings, values and norms are eventually constructed with others. This process starts from birth via imitation and mirror processes that are important foundations for sociality providing a basic sense of social connectedness and mutual acknowledgement with others. Nevertheless, these basic mirroring processes are necessary, but not sufficient, to account for the early development of reciprocal exchanges that takes place from the second month on. Imitation and emotional contagion, taken literally as close-loop automatic mirror systems, are soon transformed into dynamic, ultimately creative exchanges that take the form of open-ended proto-conversations ruled by principles of reciprocation, and develops as negotiation and mutual recognition.

As we intended to show, from the second month, mirroring, imitative and other contagious responses are by-passed. Neonatal imitation gives way to first signs of reciprocation (primary intersubjectivity), and joint attention in reference to objects (secondary intersubjectivity). From 20 months, we proposed a third level of intersubjectivity, that is the emergence of values that are jointly represented and negotiated with others, as well as the development of an ethical stance accompanying emerging theories of mind from about four years of age. The tertiary intersubjectivity is an ontogenetically new process of value negotiation and mutual recognition that are the cardinal trademarks of human sociality.

(Rochat et al., 2009, p. 14)

Implications for early years practice

I am not sure that there are direct implications other than that knowing some of this might help you interpret what you see and hear, particularly when you are working with babies and toddlers. As the authors so clearly show, very young children make extraordinary attempts to communicate, negotiate, share and make sense of the world and social interactions.

See also: Attention, cognitive development, collaborate, guided participation, meaning, relationship

📖 *Annotated further reading:*

Rochat, P., Passos-Ferreira, C., and Salem, P. (2009). Three levels of intersubjectivity in early development. In *Enacting intersubjectivity. Paving the way for a dialogue between cognitive science, social cognition and neuroscience.* Como: da Larioprint, pp. 173–190. Available at: www.academia.edu/481597/Three_Levels_of_Intersubjectivity_in_Early_Development

Download a free copy of the article by Rochat et al. It is scholarly, interesting, clearly written and accessible. Highly recommended.

Language acquisition

Synonymous with: Language development

Words or phrases linked to this concept	What it means	Why it matters
Linguistic symbols	The alphabet or characters and sounds that make up a language	Essential for communication with other speakers of that language
Rule-bound	It is held together by rules e.g. instead of like a sentence is made of subject, verb, object	In order for language to be shared there must be rules governing how it works so that there is a shared understanding
Symbolic act	Where one things stands for another	Language involves using symbols arranged to form words that can be written or said and each stands for an object or an idea or an action
Over-generalising the rules	To think that if there is a rule it must always apply	More sophisticated thinking allows us to know there are exceptions to rules
Language Acquisition Device (LAD)	The system of rules for language	The first attempt to apply a genetic explanation to language acquisition
Language Acquisition Support System (LASS)	The system of rules for language between two or more people	Recognising the importance of the context and of culture

This is, as you will appreciate, a significant and complex area of study and we will only be touching on some main themes, but you will find details of writers and experts in the field if you develop an interest in it. I find it all very fascinating.

From very early on human infants show a unique communicative pattern of behaviour. They begin to indicate the need to have things labelled or named for them. They do this by looking or eye-pointing, finger pointing or holding up objects, all aimed at inviting others to share attention and provide the label. Children begin using *linguistic symbols* (sounds and words, for example) to communicate. There is almost certainly some imitation involved as the child repeats words used by adults, then internalises the sounds heard to be able to make those same sounds in order to share meaning. Imitation is certainly an important part of beginning to speak your own language but it cannot account for certain things.

Spoken language is a *symbolic act*. Often people think of symbols being things that can be seen or touched or held or moved. Talk consists of sounds and these are not random or haphazard but combined in particular ways in order to represent things. You will know that names or nouns represent or stand for objects or people and these are the first linguistic symbols children use. Nouns are then combined with other words in order to create strings of words, then phrases and sentences. Language is *rule-bound* so that the ways in which words can be combined in order to create meaning are both clear and clearly understood by language users. But language is fluid, changing and creative. Children play with language just as they play with objects. The Russian linguist Chukovsky (1928/1963) wrote a fascinating little book called *From Two to Five*, which is full of the funny, perceptive and inventive things that Russian children said, revealing their abilities to use language creatively. If you can find a copy buy it and read it.

Noam Chomsky, an American thinker and writer who is still alive, was the first to suggest that language acquisition is genetically determined. He believed that the human infant was born pre-programmed to work out the rules of speech. If you think about it you will realise that speech – in any language – must be rule-governed if people are to be able to understand it, use it and be understood. The rules relate to the grammar of any language. In English, for example, there are rules about the order of words. We can say 'the dog jumped over the fence' but if we say 'the fence jumped over the dog' it makes no sense because a fence cannot jump. If we say 'the jumped fence the over dog' we are uttering a string of exactly the same words but in an order that prevents it from being meaningful. The same rule does not necessarily apply to other languages. In English we have rules about how we use verbs when we talk about the past tense. So we say 'we walked' and 'we talked': the rule being that we usually add 'ed' to the end of the verb. We have rules about how to talk about more than one object. So we talk about shoes and socks and pens and pencils. The rule here is that we usually add the letter 's' to the end of a noun to make that noun plural. You, as a fluent speaker of the language, will know that there are exceptions to the rules. And this is where Chomsky's brilliance emerged. We fluent speakers of the language say 'went' instead of 'goed' and 'flew' instead of 'flied'; we talk of 'sheep' instead of 'sheeps'. Chomsky noticed that young children, having started out by saying things correctly through imitating what they heard adults and fluent speakers say, move on to making mistakes by applying the rules to all situations. The way in which he described this was that the children were *over-generalising the rules*. He used this as evidence that children are brilliant thinkers, working out the patterns they hear to make up the rules and then, logically, applying them to all situations. So if we analyse this in terms of dialogue we find that the children, through their many interactions with fluent speakers of their language, adult and children, are raising questions about how language works. These questions are implied rather than spoken, but the fact that children change their verbal behaviour suggests that they are inventing theories to explain what they are noticing. Chomsky believed that it was these errors that reveal that children must have something that allows them to use the patterns they hear to work out the rules. What he proposed was that the structure of language, by which he meant the rules that bind it together to make it meaningful, depend on what he called a *Language Acquisition Device* (LAD).

Many theorists now accept that all children are potentially competent users of language from birth. When Chomsky used the term competence he meant the capacity to access the underlying and subconscious knowledge of the rule system for generating language. He believed that human infants were born with this. The errors or the mistakes children make show us the efforts they are making to find the patterns in the particular language, to work out the rules and apply them.

Case study/example

Fifteen-month-old Antonio points to the plastic farm animals he is playing with and says 'cows, horses, sheep'.

Here you can see that this very young child is imitating the correct form of plurals he has heard the fluent speakers in his world use. He has not yet worked out the pattern that operates in English for making plurals. One might say that he is 'just copying'.

But at the age of three Antonio points to the plastic sheep and labels them 'sheeps'.

He has moved on from making a grammatically correct response to making a mistake. Chomsky believed that this was because Antonio had always been paying attention to what he heard, as all human infants do. At first when he spoke he copied the models he had heard. He had always heard of sheep and never of sheeps. But with experience he worked out that adults have a pattern for making plurals: they add an 's' at the end of the word. At first Antonio used this pattern or rule to form all plurals: he has not yet learned what we know – that there are often exceptions to the rules. The consequence is that he over-applies or overgeneralises the rule to all situations. No amount of correction at this stage will enable him to rectify his errors. It is only when he has discovered that there are rules and exceptions to rules that he will be able to use both forms. In other words, only with experience of listening to experienced others will he self-correct.

Bruner saw a gap in Chomsky's theory and that gap was the lack of any reference to other people, which means a lack of reference to interaction, society, culture or context. For Bruner the development of language requires at least two people involved in negotiation. The purpose of language is communication and it is through communication that meaning is made and shared and fine-tuned. So, building on Chomsky's LAD, Bruner proposed a more sociocultural model, which he called the *Language Acquisition Support System* (LASS). Children learn their language through their interactions with others, who cue the children's responses and share meanings with them in particular contexts and within cultures. So Bruner adds a sociocultural dimension to Chomsky's model.

In his own words

Language is an essential tool – spoken language, sign language, English, Arabic – all means of making and sharing meaning. I want to quote here the words of Kornei Chukovsky (1963, revised 1968) because they give you some sense of the power of language and the genius of human infants in learning it.

> Among the early acquisitions of the child's mind, the one having the highest value is his treasure of words and grammar. He himself hardly notices the gigantic effort he is exerting while he accomplishes this learning so systematically, expediently and expeditiously. Nevertheless, an irreproachably correct mastering of speech is for many children a great ambition and joy ... [this] confirms the believe that this feeling is widespread among children 'from two to five.'
>
> I first came across an amazing example of it when Yurik, two and a half years old, once made a slip of the tongue and said instead of 'screw' –'shew'. When corrected, he said, unabashedly:
>
> 'Boria said "shew" but Yurik said "screw".
>
> This Yurik did not number among his acquaintances a single Boria. He invented a Boria for the express purpose of pinning on him all his mistakes and blunders, crediting himself only with faultless speech.
>
> (pp. 14–15)

Implications for early years practice

Most important is to remember that all languages can be used to make and share meanings. No one language is better than another. All young children learn, without having lessons, to speak their own language and often to speak more than one language. This is an astounding achievement and one that demands respect. Do ensure that you do not make comparisons or judgements but see all the children as meaning-makers and meaning sharers. Provide a language and a languages-rich environment where you have books and stories and alphabets in the languages of the children in your group. Make the singing of songs, the chanting of rhymes, the reading of stories an essential and high profile part of every day. Bathe activities in spoken language.

 See also: Becoming a reader, becoming a writer, cognitive development, formats, scaffolding learning, Zone of Proximal Development

 ## Annotated further reading:

Chukovsky, K. (1928/1963/revised 1968). *From two to five*. Translated and edited by Miriam Morton. Berkeley, LA and London: University of California Press.

This is a delightful and hugely entertaining book but it is not really about language acquisition. Much of what is written about language acquisition is technical and fairly hard going. There is some information in the 'Introducing...' series that you might find helpful.

Maintaining languages and culture:

The importance of this to learning and identity
See also key concepts: Agency, becoming a reader, bilingualism, culture, guided participation, identity, language acquisition, mark-making

Mark-making

Synonymous with: Writing, drawing, graphic skills

Words and phrases linked to this concept	What it means	Why it matters
Transcription	The ability to know how to write words and build them into sentences: the how of writing	In order to communicate the skills of writing must be acquired
Composition	What the writing will be about	All writing must be about something
Emergent writing	Children using what they know to communicate	Shows us exactly what they know, what rules they have worked out

In the developed world there is an emphasis on wanting young children to learn to read and write before they have had time to make sense of what reading and writing are for, who does them and how they are done. This emphasis on formal learning makes no sense when we think about how brilliant young children are at using everything they can to make sense of the world. In this section I am going to talk about what young children do if you remove the pressure to 'get it right' and focus on understanding what questions the children have raised and tried to answer when they do what used to be called 'emergent' writing.

We live in a literate and visual society where writing is encountered everywhere in the everyday lives of us all: adverts, text messages, emails, books, posters, leaflets, a prescription from the doctor, a birthday card through the letter box, magnetic letters on the fridge, a parking ticket on the car. Children try to make sense of this and do it by watching, listening, looking out for patterns, finding the rules and playing at writing just as they play at being the teacher or an artist or a hero. In their play they often include writing as they attempt to work out what the rules are and how writing works as a way of sharing thoughts.

A wonderful study was done by Ferreiro and Teberosky in 1979 when they studied pre-school children in Latin America to discover what hypotheses they created about writing as a system. The children, for example, believed that something very big like an elephant would have to be represented by a very big word, whereas something small like a mouse would be represented by a small word. So word size was related to object size. They also believed that for something to be a word it had to have a minimum of three letters and all three had to be different. Were they right?

Much has been written about what we, the adults, can learn from what children do if we provide opportunities for them to be writers. Do look out for the writing of such people as Margaret Meek, Frank Smith and Myra Barrs for alternative views of how to promote literacy.

We know that children start exploring signs and symbols within the context of their social and cultural lives. Where a child encounters adults who are interested in what she is doing, treat her as an equal partner in any exchange and recognise and value the cultural and linguistic input the child brings from home, this 'active, thinking, hypothesising child' (which is how she is described by Whitehead, 1990) can try out her developing ideas about writing through play. Involved in writing are the skills of *transcription* – what you need to do physically to make the marks on paper. This refers to the rules of written language – things like how words are spelled, that sentences end with full stops and that a question ends with a question mark, for example. And there is the skill of *composition* – deciding what to say and how to say it. This is what Myra Barrs (1991) called 'the tune on the page'. If we allow children to explore writing through play we find that they explore all of these aspects of written language.

The earliest thing that children explore is what they need to do physically in order to make marks on paper. Even at the age of two or three young children demonstrate that they will use different physical movements for writing from those they use for drawing. Karmiloff-Smith (1994) observed that very young children, asked to act like someone drawing, used large movements, keeping the crayon close to the paper. When asked to 'write' they tended to make smaller marks and lift the tool from the paper.

Case study/example

As children start to explore the conventions of making marks, which for them represent writing – which means that they intend them to be writing – they start to explore the arrangement of the letter shapes on the paper. Very early writing appears to cover the page randomly, sometimes going from left to right, sometimes from top to bottom, sometimes around the edges of the paper. Remember that the rules regarding the direction in which print should go will vary from language to language. Not all languages go from left to right and from top to bottom of the page.

Themba said that this was writing and not drawing

Children also play with purpose and audience. Ben wrote what he said was 'a shopping list' and later allowed his grandmother to put what he called 'proper' writing next to his invented symbols.

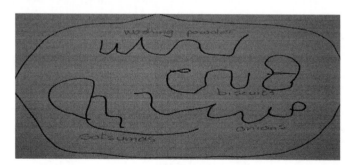

Ben's shopping list

Abiola found an envelope and put some marks on it, telling her mum that it had to be posted. She used many intricate letter-like symbols and her writing went from left to right and top to bottom, resembling the way in which an envelope might be addressed.

14/3/00

Abiola's envelope

Source: All drawn from Smidt (2011), pp. 88–90

In her own words

Glenda Bissex starts her book about how her son Paul became a writer like this:

> Five-year-old Paul was in the house. I was outside on the deck reading. After he had tried unsatisfactorily to talk to me, he decided to get my attention a new way – to break through print with print. Selecting the rubber letter stamps he needed from his set, Paul printed and delivered this message: RUDF … Of course, I put down my book.
>
> He could put his words on paper. Since literacy has become commonplace, we do not often wonder at the power of the written word, except as we may see a child come into the power that was once the secret of the priests. For the next month Paul wrote avidly, developing an alphabetic spelling system that served his needs, and producing a variety of forms (signs, captions, notes, statements, lists, directions, a game and a story) […] Paul lived in a house that was full of print and he frequently saw his parents reading and writing. We had read aloud to him almost nightly since he was old enough to enjoy a story … and he had a collection of his own books.
>
> (Bissex, 1980, p. 3)

Could you understand Paul's message? The book his mother wrote is called *GNYS AT WRK*.

Implications for early years practice

Treat the children as serious meaning-makers and set up contexts where writing for their own purposes can take place. So in the home corner place some resources that relate to reading and writing, ensuring that you reflect the languages and cultures of the children – things like magazines, recipes, paper and pencil by the phone, tablets and keyboards. Offer easy access to mark-making materials and make them freely available.

 See also: Becoming a reader, cognitive development, documenting children's progress, meaning, play

 ## Annotated further reading:

Bissex, G. (1980). *GNYS AT WRK: A child learns to write and read*. Cambridge, MA and London: Harvard University Press.

For me this was a life-changing book and I do recommend it. It is about a privileged child but it gave me a window into knowing how to decode and analyse children's mark-making.

Smidt, S. (2011). *Playing to learn: The role of play in the early years*. London and New York: Routledge.

Meaning

Synonymous with: Make meaning which means make sense of; share meaning which means come to understand with others; transform meaning which means change meaning

Words or phrases linked to this concept	What it means	Why it matters
Multimodally	Using lots of different ways of expressing ideas	Synonymous with the Hundred Languages of Children
Metaphor	Comparing one thing with another	A higher order thinking skill

You will know that young children are immediately and constantly involved in making sense of their world and of the objects, events and people in it. You will also know that Vygotsky, Bruner and others adopted a sociocultural approach to learning and development. I have chosen to look at children's drawing and this requires that I must understand the context in which children draw and see that as the point of departure for understanding what, why and how they draw. From a sociocultural perspective the relationship between adult and child in drawing was described as 'guided reinvention of knowledge' by Gordon Wells (1986), as 'negotiation of shared understanding' by Trevarthen (1995) or 'the co-construction of meaning' by Schaffer (1996). The children in these descriptions are all actively involved in interpreting or making sense of what the adults around them are doing, asking and expecting. Bruner said that meanings 'have their origins and their significance in the culture in which they are created' (1996, p. 3). The culture can be the close context of the home or the wider culture of the setting or classroom.

Dyson (1993), Kress (1997) and Pahl (1999, 2001), all interested in literacy, have offered ways of looking at drawing within studies of literacy development. Dyson, for example, looked at how children use drawing as part of developing a sense of other symbolic systems like alphabets; Kress, on the other hand, studied emerging literacy through semiotics. He saw drawing as sign making and part of the child's need to use everything to hand to make meaning. Kate Pahl and John Matthews — a distinguished artist himself – also looked seriously at drawing as part of the way in which children explore, express and share meaning.

Case study/example

Kathy Ring (2006) looked at seven children in the North of England in the context of their homes, pre-schools and schools in her study. The children were four years old and she collected drawings and photographs, talked to the children and the adults and observed. She was interested in how the mothers, in particular, offered a context for the drawing that was imbibed in some way by the children. This is a tiny study but offers some interesting insights into how these children, using the cultural tool of drawing to make sense of their world, responded to the subtle ways in which the adults involved contributed or influenced the meaning-making process. Below is an extract from Ring's own analysis of something that happened that she found interesting.

In her own words

(One) mother's role included her tolerance of what Pahl calls 'purposeful mess' (1999, p. 104), her organisation of space and time, her control over the availability of cultural objects and artefacts, including the watching of television and videos, and, importantly, her recognition of children's need to have some time relatively free from adult direction. The mothers in the study who accepted and encouraged a child's imaginative interweaving of reality and myth, answering his or her questions with warmth and good humour and responding uncritically to the products of their meaning-making, encouraged their child to experiment and communicate openly whilst de-emphasising the need for him or her to be perfect. Within the study a mother supporting a playful approach to meaning-making led, in relation to drawing, to a child acting unselfconsciously, without fear of criticism.

(Ring, 2006, p. 74)

Everyday wisdom would suggest that we become meaning-makers and narrators through imitation or copying the models around us. Kress argues – and I agree with him – that no child ever copies. What we all do is transform what is around us. Kress uses the example that follows to explain this: A three-year-old child walking up a steep hill with his family described the hill as being 'heavy'. In Kress's transformative view of meaning-making he suggests that the child, not having the correct word in his vocabulary compared his feelings about climbing the hill with other physically difficult things he had tried to do – perhaps carrying something heavy – and used that word to describe his feelings. And here is another example. Sammy, aged about four, wanting to say something important to her, said 'I want to make a proclamation'. She had, perhaps, heard a story in which the word 'proclamation' had been used and she adopted that word to describe something she wanted to do.

The children had added words to their vocabularies and imbued the words with new meanings. Heavy for one child now implied not only weighing a lot but difficult; a proclamation for the other implied something that other people do but that I can do too. Both children have transformed their own language. What matters here is that the child, in each case, has used the incorrect word but in a sense that does not really alter the meaning. You will recognise that the word 'heavy' was used not to describe the hill but the effort required to climb it: effort is always required in dealing with heavy things. Sammy did not ask for a proclamation for supper or to go on a proclamation, she used it to describe an intended action. For Kress, seeing meaning-making as being transformative allows us to explain how we each make our own route into language as we do into all other cultural systems. We might all arrive at standard English (or whatever its twenty-first century equivalent is), but we will all get there by different and personal paths.

Children, making sense of the world and keen to represent their ideas and thoughts and feelings in order to share them with others, do this in different ways, using different materials and means. Children use things they find to represent other things. Children throughout Africa use bits of wire and bottle tops and other found materials to make toys, often with moving parts. Children draw with their fingers on misted surfaces, with twigs in the wet sand on the beach, with chalk on the pavement. They use string and cardboard and glue and scraps of fabric to make cars and parachutes and human figures and boats. Children are making their own signs and in doing that they use what is to hand and what they use sometimes suggests other possibilities. Paper can be cut and folded, painted, written on, cut out, stuck to and so on. Children, in Kress's terms, act multimodally in the things they use and the objects they make and in the use of their bodies. Some aspect of their perception of a person or a place or an object features in what they make and for them this is enough to turn what they have made into that object.

Implications for early years practice

Since young children are curious, questioning and trying to make sense of the world you need to provide opportunities for them to do just this. Set up things that interest and challenge them. Find out about their interests and try to use these as starting points. Offer as many different ways as possible for them to express their ideas: writing, drawing, making, modelling, three-dimensional work, painting, dancing, making music, moving, building, narrating, cutting and sticking and whatever else you can think of. Pay attention to what children do as they work and invite and allow them to not only represent but also to re-represent.

 See also: Active learner, agency, becoming a reader, becoming a writer, collaborate, complex environments, culture, DAP, interaction with others, language, monologues, play, representation

Annotated further reading:

Ring, K. (2006). What mothers do: Everyday routines and rituals and their impact upon young children's use of drawing for meaning-making. *International Journal of Early Years Education, 14*(1), 63–84.
This is readable and includes a lot of background material in support of the things she wants to say.

Kress, G. (1997). *Before writing: Rethinking the paths to literacy*. London and New York: Routledge.
You may want to also read this book by Kress (1997).

Meaningful contexts:

An activity or experience where the purpose is clear to the child. Counting the numbers of plates to put out on the table makes sense; one plate for each person. Colouring all the big circles green and the small circles yellow has no purpose – other than to please the teacher
See also key concepts: First-hand experience, guided participation

Mediation:

The use of cultural tools made by people to interpret and explain the world
See also key concepts: Active learner, apprentice, cognitive development, collaboration, culture

Memory in action:

Bruner said that play was memory in action, which means that where the child has chosen what to do – i.e. is playing – she is able to draw on her memories to help her answer questions, solve problems or express her feelings

See also key concepts: Play

Monologues:

Talking aloud/egocentric speech

Synonymous with: Outer speech, talking to oneself, egocentric speech

Words and phrases linked to this concept	What it means	Why it matters
Signalisation systems	The systems we use for communicating with one another	We have many ways of making and sharing meaning. Language is one
Inner speech	When the child has direct access to remembered events and no longer has to speak out loud	This is really when the child can think and does not have to act out or experience or say aloud
External speech Egocentric speech	Both are synonymous with monologues or outer speech	The child says aloud what he is doing as an aid to being able to remember
Consciously	Being aware of something	An essential part of being a successful learner
Internalised	When the child has direct access to remembered events	Part of almost all learning situations

Vygotsky regarded language as the most significant of the 'complex *signalisation systems*'. What he meant was that language is the main way in which we share our thoughts and ideas with others. He set out to understand and explain the explicit and deep connection between speech and thought. Do you believe that you can think without language or that you can speak without thought?

External speech – saying things out loud or talking to oneself – comes first. This is often called monologuing and it plays a powerful role in learning and development. It is neither random nor useless. As you read through the example think about what the child is doing and why.

Case study/example

Three-year-old Leanne was drawing with felt pen on green paper, on her own, in the writing corner of the nursery classroom. She began by drawing an enclosed oval shape. She then proceeded to fill the shape with dots, some of which, as her arm descended with some force, became more extended marks. As she continued, she began to talk to herself, unaware that I was listening. [I was observing some other children at the time.] She identified the shape as a duck pond and the marks she was making as ducks. She then made a final dot within the shape, and declared it to be the plug where the water goes out. She moved to the corner of the page where she made some individual shapes working from left to right. Reaching the edge of the page she continued immediately beneath. As she did this she said slowly, as she was making the marks, 'To Auntie Bonny'.

(Cox, S., 2005, p. 118)

The running commentary indicates exactly what the child was noticing about what she was doing and why. This outer speech is social in origin in that the child is communicating with others as she uses it. It is sometimes called egocentric speech – a term I dislike since it implies that it is all about the individual child when, in effect, it is the child making what she is thinking and saying available to others.

Vygotsky believed that inner speech develops when external speech becomes internalised. This suggests that the process is that the younger or less experienced child must first think out loud before being able to think without the support of speech. Many theorists believe that the same is true of memory: once something has been enacted and remembered it is internalised. Language can now be used to reflect on action and develop thought rather than being a precursor for thinking. Put more simply, children become able to use speech and language as tools in their problem solving because speech allows them to reflect on or consider what they are doing. It is only when this outer speech becomes internalised (which means it may no longer be spoken or evident to anyone other than the child) that the child uses it privately, internally and *consciously* to solve problems.

In his own words

Vygotsky's original work was in Russian and was written in extremely dense academic language. It is difficult to read even in translation and I am not suggesting you read his work but here are some of the things he said about inner and outer speech:

External speech is a process of transformation of thought into words, its materialisation and objectification. Inner speech is a process of the reverse direction going from without to within, the process of evaporation of speech.

(Vygotsky, 1939, p. 196)

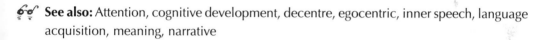 *Implications for early years practice*

If you are involved with younger children you will almost certainly hear their monologues as they seek to make meaning of the things they do and encounter. It is important to pay attention to what you hear and to use it to help you understand what the child is paying attention to, interested in or questioning. Like the errors children make, the things they say give you a window into their developing thinking. When you are with older children you are less likely to hear monologues but you should still be alert to any evidence you intuit of their inner speech – what they are thinking. Again you do this by considering carefully what their behaviour suggests they are interested in, paying attention to or questioning.

See also: Attention, cognitive development, decentre, egocentric, inner speech, language acquisition, meaning, narrative

Annotated further reading:

Smidt, S. (2009). *Introducing Vygotsky: A guide for practitioners and students in early years education*. London and New York: Routledge.

This book is written as an introduction to the complex but extraordinary ideas of Lev Vygotsky.

Multiple intelligences:

A theory developed by Howard Gardner drawing attention to the many ways in which learners express and share their thoughts and ideas.

See also key concepts: Creativity, culture, documenting, language, play, representation, roles, rules, schemas

Narrative

Synonymous with: Story making, storying

Word or phrase linked to this concept	What it means	Why it matters
Protonarrative	First stories that may not have a beginning, middle and end	Even two words linked together can be called a narrative
Narrative precocity	Means that young children surprise us with their ability to make up stories	Noticing this will raise your expectations
Correct syntactic forms	The correct use of grammar	

Human beings tend to use narrative in order to make sense of their lives. We think about what has happened and then sequence events in order that we can understand more clearly what has happened. Bruner tells us that children enter the world of narrative early in life. Those of us who have children or who have spent time with children will find this no surprise. Almost as soon as children begin to use spoken language they combine what words they have together with facial expression and gesture and intonation into tiny protonarratives. In this section you will find the examples and case studies embedded in the text rather than separated out. So here are some examples of protonarratives.

> The child looks at her empty ice cream cone and says, in a mournful tone of voice 'All gone!'

The child tells the sad story of how she has eaten all the ice cream so that now there is none left.

Arturo, given a present on his birthday, beams and says 'ammi me' (ammi is what he calls his aunt).

Arturo tells the happy story that his aunt has given him a present and he is happy.

The urge to make sense of experience through story seems to arise from the child's earliest communications with adults within the context of the culture where the intention of the adult can be seen to be narrative in the sense of turning any exchange into a story to help the infant make sense of it. One clear example of this comes from the work of Catherine Snow (1977) who, in her analysis of the speech used by mothers even in the first few months of life, noted that they commented on everyday events in a remarkably narrative way, imputing motives and emotions and the rudiments of a plot. Here are some examples supplied by students.

My husband laughed at me when I asked the baby 'Where's it gone?' when she dropped the rattle. He asks me if I think the baby knows what has happened to the rattle and if she can tell me this.

My mum says I am ridiculous when I say things like 'I know what you are smiling at!' or 'Take that grumpy look off your face'. She says it is as though I think the child knows more than she does.

Gordon Wells (1981) offered the example of a child called Mark, just short of his second birthday when they were looking at the birds outside the window and he got involved in a real conversation with his mother, taking turns and being able to comment on what the birds were doing outside his window. The conversation started with Mark drawing his mother's attention to the birds and his mother then asking him what they were doing. His answer was intelligible only to his mother 'Jubs bread' (Jubs was his word for birds). This is certainly a protonarrative but Wells tells us that only two weeks later Mark had an extended conversation with his mother and, as they talked about an imagined shopping trip, he gradually took over the role of principal narrator.

Bruner (2002) talked of the narrative precocity of infants and in doing this he cited the studies of the tape recordings made of little Emmy's musings to herself in bed before she fell asleep. The tapes were all recorded before Emmy reached the age of three. In the paper he had written with Joan Lucariello called 'Monologue as Narrative Recreation of the World' (1989) he showed how this small child used narrative. In his later book he discussed some surprising findings. For example, Emmy talked not only about the routines of the day but seemed to be very attracted by and interested in something strange or unexpected that had happened. She then mused on how she had perhaps dealt with similar things in the past or how she would deal with them if they should happen again. Bruner concluded that she was so intent on getting her story right that she seemed to have a narrative sensibility that enabled her to look for and often find the correct syntactic forms. So Bruner suggested we may have a predisposition to tell stories to make sense of reality.

It seems that the reason children become narrators is because they explore the expectations they have developed about how the world should be. They develop these expectations through their experiences and their interactions and the ways in which they look for patterns and regularities in the world. But they also love the unexpected, the fantastic and the surprise. In the stories they tell there is often an aspect of the unexpected, the unusual, the playfulness with which they view and explore the world. Here are some examples of narratives told or written by young children in which the strange or the fantastic mingle with the ordinary and everyday.

The first was told by four-year-old Octavia. It is a beautiful example of a child mixing book language and everyday language in a tiny narrative:

> Once upon a time when I was little in my garden, there were a earthworm coming out of my plant.

The second is written by Sam when she was five years old:

> This is a witch who has caught a clown and she has stuck a knife into the clown. She mixes the magic powder to kill the funny clown. She is killing him just because he is funny. But there was reason why she is going to kill the funny clown because she doesn't like funny things and all clowns are funny and specially that one. Every one liked him but that witch. Even the other witches loved him dearly. They all thought he was great except for that one who was the only witch in the wild world who didn't like funny things. She really did hate funny things …

Claudio made up a story about the witch's ball. It goes like this:

> The future can only be seen in the witch's ball. We can't see it: I don't know if I am going to be good tomorrow! To know that you have to study, to think with your head. The future is tomorrow, 'cause the glass ball shows you what there'll be tomorrow or what there was before. Witches are made like us, but they've only got one tooth – they're born like that. Now they're all dead but the glass balls are still here and that's where we can see the future.
>
> (Five- and six-year-old children of the Fiastri and Rodari Preschools,
> 2001, p. 46)

In his own words

Michael Bakhtin was a Russian philosopher and linguist and he believed, as I do, that language was dialogic, which means that it is learned and used in social contexts. He argued that every person has a unique point of view yet lives in a world of others and we experience both our own perspective and that of others in dialogue with them. These others can become the central figures or the heroes of our lives and in the stories we tell of our lives.

It is about the others that all stories have been composed, all the books have been written and all the tears have been shed … so that my own memory of objects of the world, and of life could also become an artistic memory.

(Bakhtin, 1981, pp. 111–112)

 ## Implications for early years practice

The implications relate to your awareness of and sensitivity to what children are saying and doing. Listen and look out for evidence that the child is sorting out her thoughts. Support this by the comments or gestures you make so that the child knows you are interested in what she is saying. Read to the children, tell them stories, listen to their stories. Take them to the theatre. Or even try to turn your room into one where the children make, tell and act out their own stories.

 See also: Attention, asking questions, becoming a reader, creativity, culture, DAP, documenting children's progress, interaction with others, play, relationships

 ## Annotated further reading:

Any or all of the books by Vivian Gussin Paley are wonderful, moving and easy to read. I do not recommend you try to read either Bruner or Bakhtin as they are difficult.

Neuroscience

Synonymous with: Brain studies

Words or phrases linked to this concept	What it means	Why it matters
Plasticity	Flexibility or ability to change	The flexibility of the brain is essential to learning
Neurons	Any of the impulse-conducting cells that constitute the brain, spinal column, and nerves, consisting of a nucleated cell body with one or more dendrites and a single axon. Also called nerve cell	It is the connections between these that constitute learning
Support or radial glial cells	Supportive cells that do not conduct electrical impulses but surround neurons and provide support for and insulation between them. Glial cells are the most abundant cell types in the central nervous system	Essential to the functioning of neurons
Post partum	After birth	

Note: where some terms are italicised and explained in the text they are not included in the table above.

In recent years we have been hearing and reading a lot about ongoing and recent research into how the brain works and the implications of this for learning and development. It is important to emphasise that much of the research is in its early stages, despite significant developments in techniques of imaging that allow researchers to build up a picture of the structure of the brain. So we know more than we did but we are also subject to myths about what the findings suggest.

One of the key factors emerging from recent and current research is the light it sheds on the importance of experience in shaping the developing brain. To fully appreciate the findings it is important to understand what is meant by the term *plasticity*. This can be used for two different but related meanings. The first refers to how experience shapes the brain and how changes in brain structure and function accompany learning and memory throughout life. The second refers to the brain's responses to traumatic events such as loss of sight or hearing, the amputation of a limb, the ingestion of toxic or addictive substances or other forms of brain damage.

We know that the development of the foetus may be affected by experiences with the outside world primarily through what the mother does or experiences. So what the mother eats and drinks, the stresses and emotional difficulties she encounters, any illnesses she has and what she takes into her body in the form of alcohol or drugs can all affect the developing brain. The implications in terms of poverty, deprivation, poor health, trauma and illnesses like maternal diabetes are important to consider.

Now it gets a little technical but try to follow because it is important to understand a little of the physiology. Almost all of any individual's estimated 100 billion neurons develop early in the prenatal period. They derive from neural stem cells in a process that involves both overproduction of cells and cell death. In other words there are too many of some cells and other cells die. Some researchers believe that about twice as many neurons are produced as will survive. In the outer layer of the brain – the cerebral cortex, which deals with perception, cognition and behaviour, the newly born neurons move along cells called *support* or *radial glial cells* to form six layers, each with a different function. So first the neurons differentiate into the cells that make up the cerebral cortex and then form *axons* (which are projections that send information to other neurons) and *dendrites* (which are projections that receive information from other neurons). These axons and dendrites are then able to connect to one another. The connections are called *synapses* and some of them develop during the latter part of the prenatal period, but most only develop after birth. Another process that starts at the end of the prenatal period is *myelination*, which is where axons are encased in a fatty coating that makes communication among neurons more efficient (Stiles, 2008).

The environment *in utero* is primarily a protected and safe place, although this is not always the case. It is evident that the more complex *post-partum* environment is going to play a vital role in the development of the brain after birth. Plasticity of the brain – which just means the brain's ability to change according to experience – is an important issue and there are two models for exploring the relationship of experience to plasticity and we will examine both, briefly.

The first is known as *experience-expectant plasticity* and refers to the overproduction of synapses or connections in specific areas of the brain at specific times. In the language of neuroscience these are then organised and pruned (or reduced) by experiences that are expected or common to the human species. In everyday language this means that some connections are either lost or arranged differently according to things that happen to *all* human infants. We know that almost all human infants experience changes in light and dark, hear sounds and language, have opportunities to touch and feel and move objects and learn to relate to caregivers and others. As a result of evolution neural systems in human beings expect to encounter certain stimuli in the environment in order to fine-tune their performance.

Case study/example

Think about the visual system. If the infant, through some kind of defect in the eye, cannot perceive light and dark, the development of vision will not follow the normal path. This is the result of a physical defect rather than any sort of environmental deprivation. It is important to remember that the kinds of stimuli expected vary widely so, for example, children will learn to speak their first language under a huge range of cultural conditions. Western mothers, for example, tend to talk *motherese* (or baby talk) to their infants; in other cultures mother-to-child speech is very limited. Yet babies from both systems learn to speak.

These experiences help build the structures of the brain in a way that supports particularly human physical abilities – for example binocular vision, upright locomotion, eye–hand coordination, language and emotional relationships. It is becoming apparent that human infants need to have particular experiences to enable them to: use both eyes when looking; walk upright; use their hands in a way that is coordinated with what they see; communicate with others; and experience a wide range of emotions though their interactions with others.

Now we come to one of the myths. You may almost certainly have heard of *critical or sensitive periods*, which are times when particular experience is thought to be essential for development. You will be familiar with the argument that adults find it more difficult to learn a second or additional language than children do. It was thought that this is because there is a critical period for the learning of a second language. Recent evidence shows that this is not necessarily the case. Adults, in fact, learn a second language more quickly than children, although their final level of attainment may not be as high. You will certainly have been told that the first three years of life are the most important in terms of learning. They are important, certainly, but we need to remember that we continue to learn throughout our lives.

Twardosz (2012) talks of *experience-dependent plasticity*, which involves the modification of existing synapses or the generation of new ones on the basis of *individually specific experience*. This is what enables individuals to become members of their own culture. So a child in Hanoi might eat using chop sticks, while a child in a village in the Sudan might eat with his fingers: Spanish children learn to read text from left to right while children learning Arabic learn to read from right to left. You can see from these examples how learning and memory work. Any child is born into a context of a community, a society, a set of values and customs and beliefs and traditions. The child experiences what exists within her culture. The connections in her brain are affected by what she sees and does. This experience-dependent plasticity occurs throughout life and there are no sensitive or critical periods.

This brings us to the next myth – that of the significance of providing enriched environments to young children to enhance their learning. This came from studies on rats, originally housed in sterile environments, then being given things more like what they might find in the wild. This was called an enriched environment and studies of the rats in it appeared to show some changes in brain development. The results from this were extrapolated to young children. It will not surprise you that the way in which this research was interpreted led to people in the developed world making judgements about the environments of children from poorer homes in terms of these being able to provide the children with what was deemed 'worthwhile educational experience'. It is important to remember that we cannot and should not apply findings from research on non-human species to human beings. Moreover we should always remember that what is defined as a worthwhile educational environment for the rich developed world, equipped as it will be with toys and man-made things, does not necessarily offer more worthwhile or engaging and challenging experiences than an environment set in rural or pastoral or poorer communities.

In her own words

In my view we should not remain quiet when claims that we know to be spurious are made, such as that children can organize themselves for reading and writing by pressing their 'brain buttons'.

(Goswami, 2006, p. 413)

🏃 Implications for early years practice

The only advice to practitioners is to heed this warning.

✂ **See also:** Complex or enriched environments, intersubjectivity, play, relationship

There are no recommended readings for this concept largely because everything I have read is written in such inaccessible language.

Outdoor play:

In the UK all settings offer children the opportunity to play outdoors, which allows for them to explore things on a different scale from what is possible indoors.
See also key concept: Play

Ownership:

There is much support for the autonomous child to be able to be in charge of what and how he is learning
See also key concepts: Agency, play

Painting and drawing:

Two of the expressive arts
See also key concepts: Collaboration, complex environments, creativity, culture, decentre, documenting progress, mark-making, meaning

Participation:

Joining in, working with, collaborating
See also key concepts: Agency, attention, cognitive development, collaboration, culture, expert others, imitation, interaction, intersubjectivity, guided participation, play, relationships

Peer-teaching:

Children teach one another
See also key concepts: Decentre, egocentric, expert others, intersubjectivity, scaffolding learning

Play and its role in early learning

Synonymous with: I can find no word in English that seems to mean what I think of as play. In English we use the same word for the play that children engage in and what people do with musical instruments. In many other languages, like Italian, the word for playing a game or as a child is *giocare* (related to joking and fun) and the word for playing an instrument is *suonare* (related to sound).

(In this section I am embedding all the quotations directly in the text. There is no table because the terms italicised are self-explanatory or explained in the text.)

How we define play is important because, despite the number of books and articles on the subject, it is still misunderstood. Many people think that play is something trivial, something that children can do when they have finished their work. I think that play is the work that children do as part of making sense of the world. They look, they touch, they explore and as they do this questions come to them. So they set about trying to find answers to these questions and much of what they do in their search for meaning is through play. So for me and many of my colleagues, play is a *mode of learning*. It is serious, purposeful, often sustained, possibly intense, always self-initiated and engrossing. It can be alone or with others but it is never something that someone else tells you to do.

Here is a very condensed account of the ideas of some thinkers who have influenced how we conceive of play:

- Tina Bruce talked of play being an *integrating mechanism* and what she meant was that when children are involved in doing what they have chosen to do they bring together many aspects of learning and coordinate them to create new understanding. It is the process that is important. She used the words of Paley (1981), writing about five-year-old Wally, to illustrate this:

  > He is not a captive of his illusions and fantasies, but can choose them for support or stimulation without self consciousness. He has become aware of the thinking required by the adult world, but is not committed to its burden of rigid consistency.
  >
  > (Paley, 1981, p. 8)

- Jerome Bruner saw play as a mode or a way of learning and placed importance on the process rather than the product. He talked of play being *memory in action* by which he meant that children play precisely to think about and remember events and experiences in their lives in order to make sense of them.

  > a child dropping things one after another out of the pram is not an example of random behavior but rather suggests that the child is implicitly asking a question

– perhaps 'Why do these things land on the ground? Do all things do this? What would happen if I threw it up in the air first …

(Smidt, 2011, p. 3)

- Frederick Froebel developed the first kindergarten where play was seen as the medium of education. The children were involved in manipulating objects and in craft activities, games and songs. He wanted children to achieve abstract ideas and spiritual meaning.
- Susan Isaacs was convinced that children learn best through play, which she saw as being their work. She placed some emphasis on *social interaction* in play. She was interested in the emotional needs of children and for her symbolic play and *fantasy or pretend* play offered a release for their feelings.
- Jean Piaget focused on how children make meaning through experience, in the earliest years through the *exploration of objects*. From this he thought that they began to be able to form categories and develop logical thinking. Chris Athey (1990) took his work on *schemas* further and if you are interested in this you can read her book, although it is rather difficult.
- Rachel and Margaret McMillan influenced the development of nursery education in the UK. *Outdoor play* was one of the key themes in their work and in the development of the nurseries they set up.
- Maria Montessori designed materials for the setting in which she worked and then observed the children playing with them. Her approach was very empirical, which means continually checking things against what has been observed, and some question whether she ever really recognised the significance of play.
- Janet Moyles has written much on the subject and her focus is often on the significance of the children having *ownership* of what they do. Here is what she says:

> Play in all its subtlety is not only an antidote for children being rushed through a curriculum: play *is* a curriculum and not an occasional adjunct.
>
> Children should be respected and trusted to understand the power of play in their own learning and take the lead. Practitioners should be respected and trusted similarly to understand individual children's play and learning experiences and potential and to provide an appropriate curriculum and assessment free from prescription.
>
> (Moyles in Smidt, 2010, p. 28)

- Barbara Rogoff was interested in what children do when they are on their own together, without the presence of an adult. So this interest in peer interaction is one where children are freed from adult control and can make their own choices about what to do, what rules to make and break and what to play. It was an interest very much in *social play* and involved children taking further what they had learned through guided participation. We often see children adopting the roles of the adults they have encountered as they try out what it feels like to be the teacher, the mum, the doctor, the bank manager, the baddie and more.

- Lev Vygotsky was tremendously interested in play, particularly pretend play, and saw it as *imagination in action*. So he believed that it was during play that children began to be able to move from the here and now to the what might be. He also believed that a child at play could be described as *standing a head taller* than herself and this meant that he understood that when the child was playing that child revealed more about what she knew and could do than in any other situation.

You will know that children play wherever they are and whatever their circumstances. Play is a truly universal phenomenon. Here is an example from Latin America.

Case study/examples

A 20-month-old Mayan boy was trying to decide whether or not a play dough tortilla was edible. He had been patting the dough into a tortilla with his mother's help. This is what he did:

> The baby broke off a tiny corner of the little tortilla he had made and held it up expectantly to his mother. She absently nodded to the baby as she conversed with the adults present.
>
> The baby brought the piece of play tortilla to his mouth and, looking at his mother fixedly, he stuck out his tongue and held the piece of tortilla toward it, with a questioning expression. His mother suddenly bolted out her hand and snatched his hand holding the piece of tortilla away from his mouth, blurting out 'No! Not that!' The baby looked at her with a little surprise but was not disturbed by the clear message that the dough is not edible; he watched quietly as she laughingly put the little piece of dough back on the rest of the tortilla, put it back into the baby's hand and told him that it is not to eat. He resumed patting the dough contentedly.
>
> (Rogoff et al., in Woodhead, 1998, pp. 230–1)

Some small examples from Ghana:

- From watching some of their parents in the fields the children started to ask questions about roots and this became an ongoing theme as plants were planted and dug up, some root vegetables were collected and then cooked, children took care of the vegetable patch and talked about when it might rain, what sunlight did and so on.

- A child's mother died and the teacher in the setting noticed that some of the children were re-enacting funerals and talking about death. After a long discussion with the headteacher and the child's grandmother they set up a hospital corner in the room.
- Two of the children got a new TV and were really excited about it and so the group got involved in making a TV for the classroom out of an old box and then designed their own moving pictures using rolls of discarded paper. They were very ingenious and inventive.
- The children came across the word 'pair' in their class. The language of the school was English although most of the children spoke Hausa as their first language. They struggled to understand its meaning and so the adults decided to launch a whole topic about pairs.

Implications for early years practice

Get to know the children and understand what interests them. Use children's interests to set up meaningful and challenging activities. Create a culture where children can choose what to do, with whom, how and where. Listen to them and note down significant moments. Treat play as a primary way of learning and ensure that you understand what play really means so that you can explain its significance to parents and others.

See also: Agency, asking questions, attention, bilingualism, cognitive development, collaborate, complex environments, creativity, culture, decentre, DAP, documenting children's progress, ecological model, egocentric, emotional development, expert others, feelings, first-hand experience, formats, guided participation, identity, imitation, interaction with others, language acquisition, mark-making, meaning, narrative, neuroscience, popular culture, relationship, representing and re-representing, role making and role playing, rules, and more

Note: I did not set out to ensure that play was the concept that occurs in almost every other concept in this book, but look at the list above to see how true this is. Food for thought?

Annotated further reading:

Bruce, T. (1992, 2nd ed.). *Time to play in early childhood education*. London, Sydney, Auckland: Hodder and Stoughton.

This is something of a classic and is easy to read.

Popular culture:

The entertainment that is freely available and kept up to date
Synonymous with: The culture of the streets or the everyday lives of people

Popular culture is the accumulated store of cultural products such as music, art, literature, fashion, dance, film, television, and radio that are consumed primarily by non-elite groups such as the working, lower, and middle class. This is a rather crude definition and although we might all accept that middle-class people might possibly enjoy opera more than the working-class people we cannot generalise. I am sure that some of you enjoy both high and popular culture and popular culture is the thing most likely to bond young children as a shared interest.

As with all innovations and changes there is an initial response of being wary and assuming the worst. You will hear much in the media about the negative influence of children looking at screens for too long, playing violent games, not playing outdoors with their peers and having childhoods very different from our own. In light of this a large-scale research project was carried out in 2005. This section consists almost entirely of the findings of that project.

- Young children are immersed in practices relating to popular culture, media and new technologies from birth. They are growing up in a digital world and develop a wide range of skills, knowledge and understanding of this world from birth. Parents and other family members scaffold this learning, either implicitly or explicitly, and children engage in family social and cultural practices which develop their understanding of the role of media and technology in society.
- Parents report that their young children generally lead well-balanced lives, with popular culture, media and new technologies playing an important, but not overwhelming, role in their leisure activities. Engagement with media is generally active, not passive, and promotes play, speaking and listening and reading. In addition, engagement with media and new technologies appears to be a primarily social, not individual, activity, taking place most often with other family members and in shared parts of living spaces.
- Parents are generally very positive about the role of media in their young children's social, emotional, linguistic and cognitive development. They feel that their children learn a great deal from film and television and that it has a positive impact on many aspects of their lives.
- Parents support their children's interest in popular culture, media and new technologies through the provision of resources and interactions with children (e.g. shared play, visits to theme parks) around their interests.
- Parents feel that media education should be included in the school curriculum; many think this should be so from when children are very young. Parents would also

welcome further work in schools on new technologies. They feel that this is needed in order to prepare children for the demands of the new technological age.

- Early years practitioners generally express positive attitudes towards the role of popular culture, media and new technologies in children's lives, including demonstrating positive attitudes towards their use of video/console games. However, they do have concerns about the perceived amount of time children spend on these activities.
- The majority of early childhood practitioners have used popular culture to promote learning in the communications, language and literacy curriculum at least occasionally. There is less extensive use of media and new technologies.
- Early years practitioners would like more professional development on the use of ICT, media and popular culture to promote learning in the foundation stage.
- There is disparity in the provision of resources for work on media and new technologies in maintained and non-maintained settings. Practitioners based in maintained settings reported being generally better equipped with technological hardware and software than practitioners based in non-maintained settings.
- The introduction of popular culture, media and/or new technologies into the communications, language and literacy curriculum has a positive effect on the motivation and engagement of children in learning. Practitioners report that it has a positive impact on children's progress in speaking and listening and literacy, although the present study did not include methods which could determine if this was the case.

Taken from:

Jackie Marsh, Greg Brooks, Jane Hughes, Louise Ritchie, Samuel Roberts and Katy Wright (2005) *Digital beginnings: Young children's use of popular culture, media and new technologies*, pp. 75–76.
Report of the 'Young Children's Use of Popular Culture, Media and New Technologies' Study, funded by BBC Worldwide and the Esmée Fairbairn Foundation. Literacy Research Centre University of Sheffield 2005. Available at: www.digitalbeginnings.shef.ac.uk/index.htm

Implications for early years practice

These are fairly obvious and they are to know your children and know what interests them and try to set up activities and areas of your room that allow children to reveal and develop what they know and can do. You will almost certainly have at least one surprise. I can think of one related to one of my grandchildren when he was about 11 and was with me in my car when I got lost. He took hold of my mobile phone and within minutes was directing me to the correct location. It is important to stay abreast of what interests children.

See also: Apprentice, cognitive development, culture, ecological model, play

Annotated further reading:

Jackie Marsh with colleagues has written widely and produced a number of books either as author or editor. They are all readable and interesting. My favourite is:

J. Marsh and E. Hallet (Eds), (1999). *Desirable literacies: Approaches to language and literacy in the early years.* London, Thousand Oaks, New Delhi: Paul Chapman Publishers.

Possible worlds:

The world of the imagination; the answer to questions like 'what if?'
See also key concepts: Apprentice, creativity, play

Prior experience:

What previous experience the child has had, usually, but not always referring to everyday experiences
See also key concepts: Cognitive development, complex environments, decentre, documenting children's progress, egocentric, expert others, first-hand experience

Problem posers:

Those who ask or raise questions explicitly or implicitly
See also key concepts: Active learner, agency, asking questions, culture, documenting progress, expert others, formats

Purposeful:

Where something makes human sense to the learner and she can see the purpose of doing something.
See also key concepts: Cognitive development, play

Reciprocal teaching:

Teaching which is dialogic in that both teacher and learner contribute as equals in dialogue, each being both learner and teacher
See also key concepts: Apprentice, collaboration, egocentric, expert others

Relationship, building a culture of

Synonymous with: Friendships, networks, connections, intersubjectivity
The idea of building a pedagogy of relationships came from Malaguzzi and his colleagues in Reggio Emilia and here is a summary of some of his ideas on the subject.

Those who want to work with children in a way that considers a pedagogy of relationships need to think about the following points:

A How to consider each child's reality

Malaguzzi saw each child as being essentially competent: This competence includes the abilities to communicate and form relationships. These are essential features of being human.

Case study/examples

Zeynep is integrated into a large Turkish community. She has learned how to communicate with her extended family, who speak mainly Turkish. At school the language of learning is English. In her everyday life above the dry cleaning shop. she is expected, as a girl, to help her mum in the kitchen. Her mum is a wonderful cook and is inducting the little girl in the secrets of Turkish cuisine. She sees her father reading the Turkish newspapers and listens when he and her grandfather talk about events happening throughout the Arab world. Like families scattered throughout the world events 'back home' continue to matter enormously for this little family. They are Muslim but rarely go to the mosque. They love Turkish music. The realities of Zeynep's world are multilayered and complex. She has relationships with both adults and children; with Turkish speakers and English speakers; with the expectations of home (gender-linked as in helping with the cooking and more widely to know about events in the world beyond her home) and expectations of learning (to become able to read and write; to be polite; to help in the classroom).

Those working with young children and thinking about developing a pedagogy of relationships need to know as much as possible about the lived lives of the children so that they understand the complex networks of relationships, communication skills and cultural contexts. They need to know but not to make judgements.

B   How to consider each adult's reality

The adults working in any setting are also unique individuals, each with a history and relationships with others, some intense and deeply personal, others less so. For Malaguzzi their well-being, sense of purpose, understanding of pedagogy and experience are priceless and essential to what happens within the settings. In Reggio Emilia there is no set curriculum and no targets for children to reach. All the adults in the setting are called teachers and they use what they learn during their in-service training, together with the attentive and analytical observation of what the children are doing, saying and paying attention to as the basis for setting up and resourcing the activities and planning outside visits.

Note: You have encountered Luigi earlier in this book in the section on collaboration. Here his interest in the birds is used to help understand the reality of what the adults do to extend learning.

Case study/example

In one of the Reggio Emilia settings four-year-old Luigi told one of the adults that the birds outside the window looked bored. When the teacher responded by asking why he thought they were bored he said that they don't have anything to do. The teacher listened carefully, took notes and began to think about where to take this. Luigi has expressed a concern about something he has noticed. The adult interpreted this as the child empathising with the birds and internally both raising and answering questions about why this might be so. She decided to take this further, thinking that there was potential in this for much learning – and not only for Luigi. Luigi was invited to tell some of his friends what he was thinking. The other children were interested and a lively discussion took place with the teacher sitting by, taking notes, sometimes contributing, always ready to respond to what was said. The children decided that what the birds needed were things to play on – the sort of things they found in the parks and gardens and squares of Reggio. They decided they would plan and build playground equipment for birds.

They visited a local playground, taking their drawing materials with them so that they could draw the equipment there. On their return they went out into the garden to choose a possible site for their bird playground. They began to design and draw the things they would make – swings, slides, a roundabout, a climbing frame, a bench to perch on. They then discussed and asked the teacher to make a list of what materials they might need. The list included wood, glue, string, wire, empty cartons, paper clips and more. In the days that followed the children, using their drawings as plans, set about making the playground equipment. There was much discussion about how the things they were making could be made to move, whether they would be strong enough to hold the birds, how many birds could use each piece, how they would be made to stand firmly on the ground. A great deal of problem solving, measurement, estimation, exploration of balance and weight, rotation and movement, as you can see. When the playground was ready one child asked if the teacher thought that the birds liked the playground and this led to another part of the project, where the children began to keep watch on the bird playground, taking turns to count (using a simple system of tallying) the number of birds using each piece of equipment to see which was the most popular.

C The teaching/learning cycle

- The child expressed an idea: the teacher listened attentively. A dialogue followed.
- The adult suggested the child share his ideas with friends. The adult observed and recorded what happened.
- The adult arranged for the children to visit a children's playground and organised drawing materials to take on the visit.
- The adult set up possible resources for the children to use in their design and planning.
- The adult recorded what the children said they needed for the next stage.
- All worked to find the resources.
- The children worked alone or collaboratively on their items. The teacher was on hand to interact, support and record.
- Another child expressed a related interest and the planning and doing cycle started again.

The role of the teacher here is that of being attentive to what children say and do and willing to use this as the starting point for some work. During the whole process the teacher is involved as a resource: she can write for the children, help them when they encounter something they cannot yet do alone. She can interpret their questions which are not always expressed directly. She can offer words they do not yet have to describe things they want to discuss – rotation, perhaps, or balance. Most importantly she takes notes and photographs so that she has a record of the process for her own interest, to share with her colleagues and with parents and others. It is a thoroughly professional pedagogical role, respecting the children as competent little enquirers with the teacher juggling roles as an observer, follower, initiator, provider, interpreter and recorder of the narratives being made.

In his own words

Among the goals of our approach is to reinforce each child's sense of identity through a recognition that comes from peers and adults, so much so that each one would feel enough sense of belonging and self-confidence to participate in the activities of the school. In this way, we promote in children the widening of communication networks and mastery and appreciation of language in all its levels and contextual uses.

(Malaguzzi cited in Edwards et al., 2011 p. 45)

 Implications for early years practice

While most of you will be bound by a relatively fixed curriculum there is still much to learn from this model. You cannot dispute the significance of other people to children's learning, and thinking about what children are interested in is something we all do – or should do. You will need to document carefully to persuade others that the children are learning and making progress. Gently, gently it might be possible to move slightly away from preparing children to meet targets to preparing them to be lifelong learners.

👓 **See also:** Cognitive development, collaborate, complex environments, culture, children's progress, emotional development, formats, guided participation, identity, interaction, neuroscience, play

📖 *Annotated further reading:*

Edwards, C., Gandini, L. and Forman, G. (Eds) (2011). *The hundred languages of children: The Reggio Emilia experience in transformation* (3rd edn.). Santa Barbara, Denver and Oxford: Praeger.

Much has been written about Reggio Emilia and most of it is accessible.

Representation and re-representation

Synonymous with: The Hundred Languages of Children

Words or phrases linked to this concept	What it means	Why it matters
Symbol	Something that represents or stands for something else or is combined with other symbols to make a sign. Letters of the alphabet are symbols	Part of the system of semiotics
Signs	A sign is something that stands for or represents an object or an idea. A triangular sign in the UK represents danger	Part of the system of semiotics (see below)
Semiotics	The study of symbols or signs	Much of what children learn at school involves the use of signs and symbols
Ideational function	Language used to describe or consider their experience	Children make something in order to communicate ideas about the world and the people in it. They choose the materials and the language itself. So they can write, speak, draw, build, dance, sing, act and more
Interpersonal function	The rules or laws of the chosen language relating to moods, styles and extremes	
Textual	The way in which something is represented in terms of the choices made by the maker	

In order to understand more about how children, as thinkers, represent themselves, their world, and their place in it, you need to know something about signs, symbols and semiotics. Halliday was interested in the role of signs and in how we represent ourselves to others when we communicate and he came up with three functions:

1. The first was what he called ideational – by which he meant the way we say something about the world through an object.
2. Then there is the interpersonal function where we say something about the object's relationship to the world.
3. Finally there is the textual function, which means how the sign is made.

Case study/example

Kate Pahl (1999) analysed a shopping basket made by Lucy out of an old tissue box. The ideational aspects are the objects the child said she had made, the shopping basket and list, which both arose out of the experience of playing in a shopping project in the nursery. The interpersonal aspect is the sign's relationship with the outside world and Lucy used spoken language to say that she had done the writing for her mum. The textual function is what the basket was made of – an empty tissue box, masking tape and string.

In coming to understand children's representations it is important to remember that, for the child, there is no distinction between the different ways of representation – drawing, writing, playing, constructing, making models, etc. For the child something – a question, a feeling, an idea – is the starting point for an exploration or investigation and one thing leads to another.

For both Kress and Pahl the signs that the children produce as they make models are intimately linked to their culture and their society and are also a precursor to literacy. We find children painting and modelling as ways of communicating their complex ideas before they arrive at literacy. It is worth reiterating that when children draw, paint or make models they draw on their particular cultural tools and their individual or collaborative experiences. Children making things in South Africa use what is to hand and may make wheeled toys out of pieces of wire, dolls out of cornhusks wrapped in scraps of fabric, necklaces out of seeds threaded together and furniture out of empty crates. Children in Mexico are influenced by the icons and images they see around them and use sheets of thin metal, brilliant colours, skeleton figures and, in some places, detailed miniature versions of people and animals sometimes set in empty nut cases.

In his own words

John Matthews, who has written in detail about young children as early mark makers, has a passion for understanding what is happening when children draw. Influenced by the work of Trevarthen, he drew parallels between spoken language and drawing in the sense of incorporating Chomsky's notion that children generate rules and use languages creatively. Just as children make novel utterances when they say things that they could not have heard from a fluent speaker, they make marks never seen before as they combine movements and sensations. In his book *Helping children to draw and paint in early childhood* (1994), Matthews looked at the development of his own child, Ben, and here is what he said:

> How then are we to understand what Ben is doing as he paints? It might be that the rhythm, intonation and communication patterns in babbling, along with individual sounds, are carried over into the first true sentences. … A similar relationship might exist between 'scribbling' and the first pictures. Is Ben 'babbling with paint'? He is obviously very involved in the painting and his whole manner suggests a commitment which would not be conveyed by mindless scribbling. What he is doing seems to be emotional. Perhaps it reflects or conveys his mood. It may help create a mood or at least intensify an existing one.
>
> He seems to bring some understanding to these art materials, and it is clear that he already knows a great deal about paint. He knows something about paint pots and brushes, he knows how to transport a paint-laden brush from the paint containers to the painting surface.
>
> (Matthews, 1994, pp. 17–18)

All human infants are exposed to sounds from birth and before birth and there is evidence that infants start to respond to music very early in life. Ilari (2002) noted that infants start to produce 'musical babbling', consisting of sounds of varying length and pitch, which seem to descend in melody but need not be imitations of anything heard. You will see here the links with mark-making and spoken language. Moog (1968/1976) noted that babies of about one-year-old showed likes and dislikes, by responding positively to songs, rhythmic words and instrumental music but negatively to sounds like those of traffic or vacuum cleaners. Older infants begin to beat or tap or clap hands to join in with musical games. They also move to music, spinning round, making stepping or dance movements. Trevarthen (1998), in his examination of how children need to learn a culture, found that mothers in many cultures sang to their children, danced for and with them and exposed them to the popular music of their time and place. He believed that children have an innate sense of musicality that allows them to communicate with others before the acquisition of speech. Music, said Trevarthen, is a communal, cultural and communicative act.

In the pre-schools of Reggio Emilia it is common to see children expressing their thoughts and feelings in more than one expressive language. In other words the children represent something by drawing it, then perhaps by making a model or acting it out. They are reflecting on their first representation and then, perhaps, changing or transforming it, in order to refine or shape their thoughts. This re-representation is both complex and sophisticated.

Implications for early years practice

Young children are fascinating to watch and listen to as they begin to try to share their ideas and feelings with others. Pay close attention to what they say and do try to keep in mind the idea of creative and questioning learners. The notion of children inventing rules, looking for patterns, trying things out, refining their work and using whatever is at hand will help you recognise and respond to their attempts with more respect. If they do something again it does not mean that they got it wrong. They are not mucking about. They are being very serious in their attempts at sharing meaning. Try to make representing and re-representing an essential part of your curriculum.

 See also: Attention, cognitive development, creativity, culture, feelings, imitation

 Annotated further reading:

Matthews, J. (1994). *Helping children to draw and paint in early childhood: Children and visual representation*. London. Hodder and Stoughton.

This is a classic book and worth owning. It shows you clearly the processes children go through in terms of how they are able to represent their developing understandings.

Role making and role playing

Synonymous with: Acting and linked to domestic and fantasy play

(Much of this section is in the form of examples of children making and playing roles. No table is needed since all the terms should be familiar to you.)

The human infant begins to define her identity by starting to see herself as unique yet connected to others. For most infants these others are members of the immediate family and, for some, the more extended family and then, perhaps the local community and neighbourhood. Here the child begins to interact with people and in doing this learns to see others as having feelings and intentions. Young children begin to pay attention to what others say and do: in part they mimic what they see and hear and they also internalise ways of acting, speaking and being. These build into a store of memories that can be drawn on in the complex scripts they will develop to play out the roles they need to play.

So the young child who starts to play at being different people is, in effect, trying out what it feels like to be in someone else's shoes.

Lilliane is playing in the garden with her younger brother Thomas. She is being the mother and he is the baby. She holds his hand very tightly in hers and tells him to walk more quickly. 'Come on!' she says, in a loud and irritable voice. 'I am sick of telling you. Come on! We are going to be late.' And she pulls his arm to hurry him along.

(Personal observation)

A very simple role play script, but what a lot is revealed. Here the child tries out what it feels like to be an adult – a mother, whose child is not walking fast enough. Lilliane is able to select the tone of voice and the speech patterns she must have heard adults (her mother and others) use when angry.

Zwelethini is the older child. Busi is her younger brother. The children live with their mother and life is hard, particularly for Zwelethini who must look after Busi, help her mother in the house, go to school and, in the afternoons, help out in the village. Zwelethini loves Busi but is envious of his status as both boy and younger child. Notice how this emerges in their play:

Zwelethini: Now I am going to be the baby and you are my big brother and you have to look after me.
Busi: Don't want to.
Zwelethini: If you want me to play with you, you must do it. I am the baby and I am crying and you must bring me some food to eat.
(Busi scrabbles in a box and brings her a handful of leaves.)
Zwelethini: You must mash this for me and feed me. I love being the baby. I don't have to do anything and you have to do all the work.
Busi: I want to be the baby now.

(Personal observation notes, 1998)

Often the first role play children engage in is playing out their domestic roles within the setting of home and family. When they start moving beyond the immediate family their play evolves to enacting more functional roles or the roles of people they encounter through their jobs – doctors, teachers, social workers, etc.

Here is an example of three children playing school. It is taken from Ann William's piece called 'Playing school in multiethnic London'. Wahida is ten and Sayeda is eight years old.

Wahida: Now we are going to do homophones. Who knows what a homophone is? No one? OK. I'll tell you one and then you're going to do some by yourselves. Like watch. One watch is your time watch, like 'What's the time' watch: and another watch is 'I'm watching you. I can see you ...'. So Sayeda, you wrote some in your books haven't you? Can you tell me some, please. Can you only give me three, please.
Sayeda: Oh, I wanted to give you five.

Wahida: No Sayeda, we haven't got enough time. We've only got five minutes
to assembly.

Sayeda: Son is the opposite of daughter ... And sun is ... It shines on the sky so
bright...

(Williams, Gregory et al., (2004 p. 63)

In this wonderful example you see Wahida using the language of the classroom and the intonation patterns used by teachers. She is clearly in control and inducts her younger sister not only into the mysteries of homophones but into the practices and language of school. Later, in the same chapter, Williams cites a pretend telephone conversation between 11-year-old Lee and 7-year-old Cathy:

Lee (pretending to phone): Hello Miss Rhodes?

Cathy (talking with an upper-class accent): Yees

Lee: Your daughter's gone on a trip and she won't be back until about 6 o'clock
tomorrow night.

Cathy: Has she now! Not again!!

Lee: I imagine she stayed overnight at school so I'm very sorry about that.

Cathy: She said she was writing a story.

(Williams, 2004, p. 60)

Children are consummate players of this game of playing at being other people. They are able to mimic the language patterns of people in authority and introduce into their role play an exploration of some of the issues that currently concern them – in this case possibly excuses, lies and explanations.

In all these examples of role play we see children involved in answering the questions they have set themselves, which appear to be of the 'What if?' variety. What if my friend is nasty to me? What if I could be the younger child? What if I felt really angry? As they play they make decisions about who and what is involved in the play, where the action takes place and what the central themes are. This requires them to develop and use a range of complex cognitive and social skills including skilful negotiation, logical sequencing of events, drawing on and combining experiences, symbolisation, speaking and listening. As they move into more abstract play the same principles apply. The children create their own scripts, negotiate about who will play what part and use whatever is to hand to represent whatever they agree on. Can we ever talk of children as just playing?

In his own words

Vygotsky (1967), writing more than 45 years ago, understood that play was one of the ways in which children make sense of their world together with their place and the place of others in it. Most significantly he, more than any other theorist, appreciated just why play matters.

In play a child is always above his average age, above his daily behaviour; in play it is as though he were a head taller than himself.

(Vygotsky, 1967, p. 16)

It is really worth thinking about this and perhaps discussing it with a friend or colleague.

 ## Implications for early years practice

Most importantly take play seriously. When children choose to adopt roles this is serious cognitive work. It is a way of addressing the many unanswered questions children raise; of working collaboratively with others, making choices and decisions; of trying what it feels like to be someone else – an adult, a baby, a teacher, a frightened person, very angry and more. Even those of us who value role play in the early years run the risk of not taking it seriously enough. Make space for it as a mode of learning in your curriculum.

 See also: Attention, cognitive development, creativity, culture, ecological model, expert others, guided participation, identity, play, relationships

 ## Annotated further reading:

Vonga, Keang-Ieng [Peggy] (2012). Play – a multi-modal manifestation in kindergarten education in China. *Early Years: An International Research Journal*, 32(1), 35–48.

This is a journal article and is a really interesting and accessible account worth reading. You can download is using this link: http://dx.doi.org/10.1080/09575146.2011.635339

Rules, making and breaking them

Synonymous with: Understanding about what is accepted and why

Words or phrases linked to this concept	What it means	Why it matters
Imperative	Something important. In this context it refers to giving an order	Rules that must be obeyed because they are really important, like 'Don't put your hand on the cooker'
Normative	Relating to the expectations or rules/norms of the situation	Rules defining what is normal, conventional or expected, like eating with a knife and fork or always saying 'thank you'

As children seek to understand the world they pay attention to the patterns they are able to discover and then generate a set of rules and test these out. We see this most clearly in analysing what children do when they first begin to use spoken language. They live in a social world and around them have models of people using their first or home language or languages. They listen, they mimic, they observe. In doing this they work out the particular rules that govern their language. At first they tend to make few errors because their first attempts at speech depend largely on copying. They say just what they hear. As they become more sophisticated they notice the patterns relating to aspects of grammar. In English, for example, the letter 's' is usually added to the end of words to create plurals. Children decide that this must be a rule and they know, from experience, that it is important to stick to the rule. So they begin to apply the rule to everything. We hear them say words like 'childs' and 'sheeps' as the plurals of child and sheep. These errors are evidence of what the children are working out.

There are rules everywhere. Within every child's home will be rules relating to what is accepted and what is not. Understanding such rules is important in belonging to a family or a group, a society and a community. In some cultures it is regarded as rude for a child to look an adult in the eyes. In some cultures children are still expected to be seen and not heard. Young children are easily inducted to the rules of their communities and cultures. They are learning about what is regarded as right and wrong.

Piaget believed that for young children all rules needed to be obeyed. The young child was not able to make moral judgements or comparisons. But later work gives evidence that even very young children can make moral judgements. Judith Smetana (1981) carried out some research with children as young as two and a half, presenting them with everyday scenarios. In some of these a child breaks a rule in the pre-school – perhaps refusing to hang up her coat, eat her lunch or tidy up at tidying up time. In other scenarios the broken rules may cause some real physical or psychological damage to the child. So here one child might be hitting or teasing another child or taking something that belongs to someone else. The children were asked how bad these transgressions were and whether the children concerned should be punished.

Smetana asked the children if the action might be acceptable if it had taken place in a setting with different rules. In other words would this action be acceptable if the rules were changed? In effect she was asking the children to decide if it would be acceptable to refuse to eat your lunch or to hit a child if the teacher or other adult said it was acceptable. Her findings were that even such young children understood the differences between breaking rules where there were no personal consequences and breaking rules where someone got hurt.

Many theorists have been interested in how children make and use rules in their play and in specifically rule-bound games, which are a feature of many childhoods. In any activity that the child has chosen and that involves pretence, the child, herself, sets and alters the rules. If, for example, she uses a block of wood as a mobile phone she invokes what she believes all mobile phones do. In other word she creates a rule. She puts the block of wood to her ear just as she has seen others do with mobile phones. Another way of expressing this is that the child has made the block of wood represent a mobile phone. The block of wood has become a symbol or sign for the child.

In their own words

Hannes Rakoczy, Felix Warneken and Michael Tomasello carried out studies with both two- and three-year-old children where a puppet called Max entered a game being played and performed some action inappropriate to the game. They looked at how the children responded to this. Here, to give you a flavour of how some of these very young children responded, is an extract from their article:

> The three-year-olds in both studies revealed a highly consistent response pattern. In response to the puppet's mistakes … they produced both distinctively normative interventions (e.g., 'No! It does not go like this!') and imperative ones (e.g., 'No! Don't do it that way!'). But they hardly did so when the puppet performed the same act in the control conditions. That is, that did not disapprove of the action just generally and for irrelevant reasons (e.g., personal preferences) but specifically only when it was a mistake. And this pattern was found both with actions that were somewhere in between purely conventional game acts and instrumental acts (Study 1) and with clearly conventional game acts (Study 2A). The three-year-olds in both studies thus revealed a clear awareness of the normativity created in simple conventional rule games: In the context of the game, the assignment of status to objects and actions licenses certain acts and makes others mistakes. Furthermore, the same act in a different context does not necessarily count as a mistake – even if the context is indicated only by the actor's announcement (to play or not play the game). The fact that the two-year-olds showed a qualitatively similar response pattern, though with less distinctively normative interventions, is plausibly interpreted as showing an analogous normative awareness as in the three-year-olds, though perhaps in embryonic form only.
>
> (Rakoczy et al., 2008)

You may have struggled with the language here so go back to the table at the beginning of this section and then read it again.

Implications for early years practice

You will almost certainly find it interesting and informative to pay attention to seeing how the children you are involved with make, adapt, change and negotiate rules and also to take notice of how they are able to make moral judgements about which rules can be broken and which not.

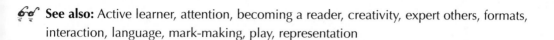 **See also:** Active learner, attention, becoming a reader, creativity, expert others, formats, interaction, language, mark-making, play, representation

📖 *Annotated further reading:*

Smetana, J. (1981). Preschool children's conceptions of moral and social rules. *Child Development*, *52*(4), 1333–1336. Available at: www.jstor.org/stable/1129527

You might try downloading this article, which is short and readable.

Scaffolding learning

Synonymous with: Supporting learning, helping the child take the next step in learning

Words or phrases linked to this concept	What it means	Why it matters
Indiscriminate praise	Untargeted praise	It shows the child how little attention the adult giving the praise is paying to what it is the child is doing
Notional gap	A gap that is not physically present	The gap between what a child can do alone and what he might do with help is not physical but abstract

One of the most important things you do as someone working or living with a young child is to support their learning. Within the home this support is something you do naturally, always in the context of something that makes human sense to the child you are with. In schools and settings it is more difficult. Faced with more than 20 children in the class or setting how can you support each one take the next step in learning?

Do you think that praise would work? Who and what would you praise?

There is a story about Adina, new to the nursery class and being looked after by Nicola, aged four. When Adina began to take her painting off the easel Nicola asked her what she was doing.

'Going to show the teacher' said Adina.

'She'll only say it is beautiful' responded Nicola.

Perceptive Nicola had noticed that there was a culture of what one might call indiscriminate over-praising in the nursery class.

Of course praise is important but indiscriminate praise is insulting to children and they learn little or nothing from it. The adult responding with a 'Lovely!' or 'Well done' does not give the child any clue as to what it is that she has done that has earned the praise.

We need to mention two theorists in connection with scaffolding and the first is Vygotsky. He thought very carefully about one of the features of early learning, which was that young children can almost always do or achieve something when they have help doing it. A novice child builder is likely to be able to construct a taller or more complex structure if she is alongside another and more expert other. He suggested that there is a notional gap between what the child could do alone and what the child could do with help, and he called this *the Zone of Proximal Development*. He was describing the distance between a child's *performance level* (or what the child could do alone) and a child's *potential level* (or what the child could do with help). Many people struggle with this because the gap is not actual or measurable. It just means that in order for a child to become an independent learner she needs to take the next step with help.

Bruner, interested in young children and learning and teaching, had read Vygotsky's work and it was he who first used the word scaffolding in connection with education. He used the analogy of the scaffolding that is put up whilst a building is being constructed or restored. The scaffold that the adult erects allows the child to take small supported steps in learning and when the child is able to manage without help the scaffold is removed.

It sounds quite straightforward but it is something that requires considerable sensitivity and skill. You might want to think about what it is that the adult or more experienced person has to do to successfully scaffold learning. The example below gives some pointers to what needs to be done for scaffolding to be successful. First you will read the notes jotted down by the teacher as part of documenting children's progress and then you will read an analysis of what the more experienced other – Marva in this case – did to scaffold Zac's learning.

Case study/example

Observation notes

Zac said he wanted to make a boat out of found materials. He spent a considerable amount of time picking up one thing, looking at it and then putting it down again. The teacher, Marva, watching him, let him carry on doing this for some time without intervening, but when she noticed that he seemed unable to make a decision she went over and asked 'Are you looking for something special? Something important? I know it is for your boat.'

'I need something that it won't matter if it gets wet' said Zac.

'Ah' said Marva. 'I understand. You want something that can go in water without getting so wet that it will sink'.

Zac nodded and smiled. Then he picked up a cardboard box. 'This would be good to put things in but if I put it in the water it is going to get too wet and soggy.'

Marva agreed and then held up an egg box. He shook his head. 'It's too small' he explained.

'Ah, you want something bigger and waterproof. Wait here for a minute. I think there are some more containers in the cupboard.'

She went over and brought back a box full of plastic food containers, shiny foil containers, plastic lids, empty cans and toilet roll holders. Zac explored each object carefully and then selected a plastic food container and set about making his boat.

Analysis of the role of the teacher

Read through the observation notes again and jot down your own ideas about what the teacher, Marva, did to support Zac's learning. Now read through this and see if you agree with Marva's analysis.

Can you see how Marva took time to understand what it was that Zac was doing? She needed to do this in order to ensure that her intervention would be useful to him. He was able to explain the problem clearly and she was then able to offer him an alternative to his first choice of cardboard box, which he rejected because it was the wrong size. This offered her the opportunity to repeat his assessment of the object (too small) and to introduce the word 'waterproof' to broaden his choice of words. You will remember he had used the words 'wet' and 'soggy'. So she paid attention to what he was doing and saying and tried to match her words and actions to what she perceived as his needs. She then provided him with some resources which he could sift through to make his own choice. So she scaffolded his learning through language (helping him vocalise his problem and enhancing his vocabulary) and through offering him resources. Finally he was able to make his boat unaided because her intervention had allowed him to make the crucial choice of container without assistance.

Marva's actions were quite simple but they were totally dependent on her being able to work out what it is that the child was interested in and in identifying what, if any, assistance he needed.

(Smidt, 2011, pp. 23–24)

In his own words

On watching a mother sharing a book with her young child Bruner wrote:

> Each step of the way, the mother incorporated whatever competences the child had already developed – to be clued by pointing, to appreciate that sounds 'stood for' things and events, etc. The mother remained the constant throughout. Thereby she was his scaffold – calling his attention, making a query, providing an answering label if he lacked one, and confirming his offer of one, whatever it might be. As he gained competence she would raise her criterion. Almost any vocalization the child might offer at the start would be accepted. But each time the child came close to the standard form, she would hold out for it. What was changing was, of course, what the mother expected in response – and that, of course, was 'fine-tuned' by her 'theory' of the child's capacities.
>
> (Bruner, 1983, p. 171–172)

It is worth reading this again because it offers a perfect description of how when one person is really paying attention to another they can tailor their responses to what they notice. It is no simple thing to do. It requires great sensitivity and awareness but it is the most effective way of enhancing learning that I know.

Implications for early years practice

If you learn nothing but this from this book it will change the way you interact with children. Scaffolding is something you do every day, with all the children at some time, possibly without being aware you are doing it. To scaffold learning you and the child need to share attention. This means you must have a very good idea of what the child is interested in, paying attention to, asking a question about or trying to achieve. When you have become aware of this you are able to scaffold. Usually you, the adult, will lead by making a comment or a asking a focused question. The child will respond and if you pay attention to the child's response you may have to adjust your expectations of the child. Each response you make gives the child something to use and either consolidate or extend her thinking. Here is an example. Read it through and think about how the feedback given relates to what the child is interested in, is helpful in terms of taking learning forward and enables the child to move from dependence to independence.

> The nursery nurse notices that a child has made a very complex model using many different resources. She sits down next to the child and starts a conversation. 'I love your model. You have used so many different things – egg boxes, toilet roll holders, lids and shiny things. Oh, and look, some buttons.'

What do you think the child gets from this adult response? Think carefully about this before reading on.

I would suggest that the child notices that the adult is really interested and not just asking questions so he joins in, saying:

> 'It took me a long time, you know.' The adult responds. 'Yes, I noticed that you were busy doing it all morning, I wonder if that was because it was so difficult to fix some of the bits together.'

Do you notice here that the adult is engaging in a proper dialogue with the child and involving the child in finding out what problems he has overcome or has yet to overcome?

> The child replies 'I used this strong glue and also some sellotape and Joshua (another child) gave me these … these … 'lastic bands and I used those'. The adult continues 'Well, you have made a really exciting model with some bits that move. Are you going to take it home?'

(Smidt, 2005, p. 55)

See also: Attention, formats, guided participation, popular culture, Zone of Proximal Development

Annotated further reading:

I am not offering any further reading here other than to suggest that you look at any of my books mentioned in this section and, if you can manage it, try reading bits of Bruner's (1983) *In search of mind: Essays in autobiography*, London: Harper Collins. You may find it a struggle as it is dense and very long.

Schemas:

Repeated patterns of action

Synonoymous with: Schemas was a term used by Piaget and I cannot think of any word that is synonymous with it.

Words or phrases linked to this concept	What it means	Why it matters
Sensory/motor	Using all senses and movements to make sense of anything	This is the way in which infants explore and make sense of the world
Symbolic/ representational	Moving into using materials to illustrate, symbolise or represent something	Children are then able to represent in some way what they are interested in
Functional dependency	Being helped to understand circularity, for example, by being shown different types or examples	Children are helped to see links between different aspects of what they are interested in
Thought	Being able to understand something without concrete experience	Children no longer need the actual object but can rely on their internalised representations
Rotation	One schema where the child is interested in the features of things that are round or circular and roll or rotate	Part of making sense of the world

Piaget conceived of cognitive development occurring through age-related stages and this view, although still influential in many schooling systems, is now largely discredited. But one of his most important ideas relates to how children organise their developing understanding of the world into increasingly complex cognitive structures. During infancy and early childhood these cognitive structures are called schemas. At first they are based on actions but later on representations and eventually they become internalised.

In their own words

Halfpenny and Pettersen (2014) give this example of a schema in practice:

> Charlie (two years, four months) has a simple schema for dogs that includes information such as 'four-legged' and 'moving'. When Charlie sees a horse for the first time, therefore, he points to it and calls it 'big doggie'.
>
> However, with experience, and parallel to Charlie's increasing capacity for classifying and categorising objects, he will learn to identify and name the many different types of animals he encounters. In this way, children's schemas are

constantly expanding and adjusting to reflect the dynamic and ever-changing nature of their understanding of the world around them.

(pp. 25–26)

A schema, then, is one of the basic building blocks in Piaget's theory of cognitive development. One of the most important books on the subject was written by Chris Athey in 1990. *Extending thought in young children: A parent–teacher partnership* is a detailed account of schemas and their relevance, but it is a difficult book to read, although certainly full of wonderful illustrations and examples of children's thinking.

Cathy Nutbrown (1994) also wrote a book on schemas, one that is more accessible. In it she drew on Athey's work and noticed that some children develop a persistent interest in something and then explore it in many different ways. Her book is called *Threads of thinking* and using the idea of thought being made up of different threads may be helpful to you in coming to understand schemas. You may have come across children whose behaviour seems strange – an overwhelming sense of the child doing something that looks random – over and over again, sometimes over weeks or months. Parents often complain that the child at home engages in this repeated behaviour, which seems to serve little or no purpose. But people who pay close attention to what children are doing find that the behaviour is not haphazard or useless but part of the child's endless search for meaning.

Case study/example

Fran Paffard, familiar with all the work on schemas, offers us the example of Sophie who, at the age of three, demonstrated her interest in and passion for rotations and circularity. Here is Fran's analysis of what Sophie was exploring. It is very helpful in getting a sense of how children who engage in schematic behaviour are actually being logical and systematic in their attempts to make sense of aspects of their world.

Sophie was involved in exploring rotation and circularity through using movement and her senses. She spent time out in the garden of the nursery chasing round the trees, spinning on an old tyre swing. Given a skipping rope she spun it round so that the rope flew out in a wide circle. In the cooking corner she used both hands to make circles in the flour in a baking tray.

She also enjoyed making representations, often involving using paper or cardboard circles, round plastic lids and corks. She liked making plasticine into balls and sausage shapes. She often mentioned how she loved round things.

> In terms of functional dependency she showed an interest in the circular clock face and played at moving the hands and using the clock to illustrate open and closed in the play shop. She was able to give an explanation for why round things roll and others don't and when some of the marbles for the marble run got lost she made balls out of plasticine. Here it is evident that she is able to reflect on or think about what she has experienced in order to arrive at some explanations.
>
> (Based on Paffard in Smidt, 2010)

Implications for early years practice

For those of you working with very young children, coming to understand the importance of schemas in cognitive development is important. Seemingly random behaviour becomes comprehensible and when you look at it in this way you will be letting the child know that you take her behaviour seriously. So, as so often, paying attention and having high expectations will allow you and the child to share a developing interest.

See also: Active learner, asking questions, cognitive development, play

Annotated further reading:

Athey, Chris (1990). *Extending thought in young children*. London: PCP.
An important but rather difficult book to read, but do look at some of the children's drawing (pages 112 to 127).

Halfpenny, A. and Pettersen, J. (2014). *Introducing Piaget*. London and New York: Routledge.
A very recent publication and part of the 'Introducing…' series.

Nutbrown, Cathy (1994). *Threads of thinking: Young children learning and the role of early education*. London: PCP.
Accessible and useful.

Paffard, Fran (1998/2010). Patterns of play: Observing and supporting young children's schemas. In S. Smidt (Ed.), *Key issues in early years education: A guide for students and practitioners* (2nd edn.). London and New York: Routledge.

Scientific concepts:

The more complex language of analysis and explanation
See also key concepts: Bilingualism, cognitive development, collaboration, first-hand experience

Scripts:

The words and actions children create for themselves and others as they explore role and rules in their social worlds
See also key concepts: Identity, role making and role playing

Semiotic:

System of signs and symbols
See also key concepts: Attention, meaning, representation

Significant moments:

When there is a noticeable leap in learning or when the child does something for the first time
See also key concepts: Documenting progress, expert others, play

Signs/symbols:

Where things are represented in some abstract way as in pictures, words, numerals, etc.
See also key concepts: Apprentice, attention, becoming a reader, cognitive development, meaning, mark-making, representation

Standing a head taller:

Vygotsky said that in play a child stood a head taller than himself, meaning that the child revealed more of what he could do than he might in any other situation
See also key concepts: Play, representation, Zone of Proximal Development

Sustained shared thinking:

When children engage with others, adults or peers, both focused on the same thing, there is likely to be a leap in learning
See also key concept: Intersubjectivity

Symbolic representation:

Where something is represented abstractly through the use of signs or symbols
See also key concept: Creativity

Theories of children:

The questions children ask and answer, developing hypotheses and theories as they attempt to make sense of the world
See also key concepts: Asking questions, creativity, documenting children's progress, intersubjectivity, language acquisition

Transforming:

Children as they make sense of the world, often change or transform things as part of the process. This is a higher level cognitive process
See also key concepts: Agency, cognitive development, collaboration, creativity, culture, meaning, monologues, representation

Zone of Proximal Development (ZPD):

The notional gap between what a child does alone and could do with help

This book ends with one of Vygotsky's key themes and one that is extremely important to anyone wanting to know more about how people teach and learn. To understand it you need to be sure that you are familiar with these concepts, already covered in this book:

- Active learning
- Agency and ownership
- Asking questions
- Collaboration
- Documenting progress, giving feedback
- Expert others, peer teaching, reciprocal teaching
- Guided participation
- Interaction
- Intersubjectivity, shared thinking
- Play
- Scaffolding learning

We start with a very simplified version of what the Zone of Proximal Development (ZPD) is and then give examples of it to clarify.

The child, living and learning alongside others, adults and peers, actively seeks to understand every aspect of her world. She develops interests or passions through her everyday experience and raises questions about the things she encounters. Does my picture disappear if I paint over it? Will this square thing roll down a ramp? Is there someone inside the television? She raises questions about the other people in her world in her attempts to understand not only objects but people and their feelings and thoughts.

Often she collaborates with others although she does some things alone. The adults in her world watch her and listen to her and talk to her. Within the close environment of home they pay real attention to her and her relationships with them are often dialogic in that they are equal partners. She learns from those with more experience – the expert others – and becomes an expert other herself as she learns and develops. All her learning is social. There are some things she can do without help but there are also things that she might be able to do with help. And it is the gap between these that Vygotsky called the ZPD.

Vygotsky had noticed that children deeply engaged in play often surprised him in terms of what they revealed they knew and could do. When children were following their own interests and passions they seemed 'a head taller' than they did doing other activities. You need to remember that the essential feature of play is that it is self-chosen and the significance of this is that it is where the child is totally involved in raising and answering questions related to what concerns, fascinates or interests her. So the child, at play, reveals much about the gap between her performance level (what she can do alone) and her potential level (what she could do with help).

It is what fills the ZPD – the gap between the performance level and the potential level – that is important. This is where the role of others in learning comes about. Sometimes the child is engaged in pretend play and the impetus of her involvement in what she is doing alone, or with others, enables her to make a leap in learning. Sometimes a more expert other offers her a physical tool, a verbal message or something else that enables her to take the next step. So the gap can be filled by play, exploring roles and rules, getting help, using cultural tools and more.

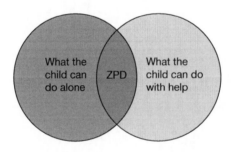

Case study/example

Six-year-old Louis was learning his multiplication tables and the teacher taught him what he called 'a trick' for working out the nine times table. For a week he spent much of his time with paper, pencil and calculator and then told his childminder, Maria Figueiredo, what he had discovered:

> Imagine you are doing 5 x 4. Now 4 is an even number, so for even numbers you break them into half and then add a zero to the number. See?
>
> He held up the paper to me so I could see his work:
>
> 5 x 4 = ?
>
> 4/2 = 2
>
> = 20
>
> Now listen carefully because the odd numbers are harder. Imagine we are doing 5 x 3. Three is the number you are going to work on, so this time you go for the number (which comes) before 3 which is 2. Then break it into half, which is 1 and add a 5 to it which makes 15!
>
> (Figueiredo, 2010, pp. 104–105)

This is a wonderful example of a child being able to explain, in some detail, the solution to a problem he set himself through what he had learned through formal instruction at school. He identified the problem and used tools including mathematical symbols (=, x, /) and language – the latter both to explain the problem and its solution and as a tool for his thinking – paper, pencil and calculator. It is questionable whether he would ever have had the opportunity in class to reveal just how much he knew. A teacher, with the pressures of many children and demands, may never find the time to invite this sort of exchange.

> A four-year-old girl is looking at a collection of shells, rocks and pebbles, untidily arranged on a table with an assortment of magnifiers of different shapes and sizes. She selects one large spiral shell and examines it closely, first with the naked eye and then with some of the magnifiers. She uses the hand lenses, large and small, moving them to and fro to get the best magnification. She bends down and puts her face right up against the lens, as if she is trying to work out the best distance between her eyes, the lens and the shell. Then she puts the shell down on the table, placing it under the magnifying glass mounted on a tripod; she leans over the tripod, satisfied she has seen all there is to see. Then she puts the shell back on the table, under the tripod, and bends

over it once more, laying her ear close to the lens, as if she were listening to the shell, through the magnifying glass.

(Drummond, 2010, p. 37)

This observation is fascinating in terms of how clearly it allows us to follow the processes this little girl goes through as she explores some objects available to her in a school environment. The educators have provided interesting natural objects together with the tools to allow further physical exploration. There is no evidence of any spoken language in this extract and the reader is left to fill in the possible thoughts going through that child's mind as she moved from one thing to another. Most fascinating is her assumption that a tool (the magnifying glass), which she realised could make things look bigger might be able to make the same things sound louder.

In each of these examples the children are using cultural tools – numerical symbols, a magnifying glass – as they explore something that interests or challenges them. Can you work out what role the more expert other – the teacher or adult – has done to allow the child to bridge the notional ZPD gap?

In his own words

We are almost at the end of the alphabet and I want to close the book with the words of one of the thinkers whose work has most inspired me. Here is what Vygotsky wrote about the Zone of Proximal Development:

Pedagogy must be oriented not to the yesterday, but to the tomorrow of the child's development. Only then can it call to life in the process of education those processes of development which now lie in the zone of proximal development.

(Vygotsky, 1993, p. 251–252)

It is a reminder to us all to think ahead rather than back in time so that the process of education focuses on how to help the learner move ahead.

Other texts mentioned in this book

Athey, C. (1990/2007). *Extending thought in young children: A parent–teacher partnership* (2nd edn.). London: SAGE.

Bakhtin, M. (1981). Discourse in the novel. In C. Emerson and M. Holquist (Eds), *The dialogic imagination: Four essays by Bakhtin*. Austin, TX: University of Texas Press.

Barrs, M. (1998). *Part to whole phonics*. Portsmouth: Heinemann.

Bronfenbrenner, U. (1973). *Two worlds of childhood: U.S. and U.S.S.R.* New York: Simon & Schuster

——(1979). *The ecology of human development: Experiments by nature and design*. Cambridge, MA: Harvard University Press.

Bruner, J. (1983). *Child's talk: Learning to use language*. New York: Norton.

——(1996). *The culture of education*. Cambridge, MA: Harvard University Press.

——(2002). *Making stories: Law, literature, life*. Cambridge, MA: Harvard University Press.

Bruner, J., & Lucariello, J. (1989). Monologue as narrative recreation of the world. In K. Nelson (Ed.), *Narratives from the crib* (pp. 73–97). Cambridge, MA: Harvard University Press.

Cox, S. (2005). Intention and meaning in young children's drawing. *International Journal of Art and Design Education*, 24(2), 118.

Darwin, C. R. (1877). A biographical sketch of an infant. *Mind. A Quarterly Review of Psychology and Philosophy*, 2(7), 285–294.

Darwin, C. (1887/1958). In Barlow, N. (Ed.), *The autobiography of Charles Darwin 1809–1882*. London: Collins.

Drummond, M. J. (2010). Under the microscope. In S. Smidt (Ed.), *Key issues in early years education: A guide for students and practitioners* (2nd edn.). London and New York: Routledge.

Dyson, A. H. (1993). *The social worlds of children learning to write in an urban primary school*. New York: Teacher's College Press.

Ferreiro, E., & Teberosky, A. (1979). *Literacy before schooling.* Portsmouth, NH: Heinemann.

Figueiredo, M. (2010). Tricks. In S. Smidt (Ed.), *Key issues in early years education: A guide for students and practitioners* (2nd edn.). London and New York: Routledge.

Five- and six-year old children of the Fiastri and Rodari Preschools (2001). *Il futuro e una bella giornata (The future is a lovely day).* Reggio Emilia: Reggio Children.

Goswami, U. (2006). Neuroscience and education: From research to practice. *Nature Reviews Neuroscience, 7,* 406–413.

Gottlieb, A. (2006). *The Afterlife is Where We Come From.* Chicago: University of Chicago Press.

Heath, S. B. (1983). *Ways with words: Language, life and words in communities and classrooms.* Cambridge, MA: Cambridge University Press.

Ilari, B. S. (2002). Music perception and cognition in the first years of life. *Early Child Development and Care, 172*(3), 311–322.

Johnson, M. H. (1990). Cortical maturation and the development of visual attention in early infancy. *Journal of Cognitive Neuroscience, 2,* 81–95.

Jones, S. S. (2006). Infants learn to imitate by being imitated. In C. Yu, L. B. Smith, & O. Sporns, *Proceedings of the International Conference on Development and Learning* (ICDL). Bloomington, IN: Indiana University Available at: www.indiana. edu/~infcomm/labwork/Jones_paper.icdl.06.pdf

Karmiloff-Smith, A. (1994). *Baby, it's you.* London: Ebury Press.

Luria, A. R. (1976). *Cognitive development.* Cambridge, MA: Harvard University Press.

Moog, H. (1968/English translation 1976). *The musical experiences of the pre-school child.* London: Schott Music.

Moyles, J. (2010). Play: The powerful means of learning in the early years. In S. Smidt (Ed.), *Key issues in early years education: A guide for students and practitioners* (2nd edn.). London and New York: Routledge.

Nurse, A. (2001). A question of inclusion. In L. Abbott and C. Nutbrown (Eds), *Experiencing Reggio Emilia: Implications for preschool education.* Buckingham: Open University Press.

Nutbrown, C. (1998). Managing to include? Rights, responsibilities and respect. In P. Clough (Ed.), *Managing inclusive education: From policy to experience.* London: PCP/ SAGE.

Pahl, K. (1999). *Transformation: Meaning making in nursery education.* Stoke on Trent: Trentham Books.

——(2001). Texts as artefacts crossing sites: map making at home and at school. *Reading: Literacy and Language, 35*(3), 120–125.

Paley, V. G. (1981). *Wally's stories: Conversations in the kindergarten.* Cambridge, MA and London, UK: Harvard University Press.

——(1988). *Bad guys don't have birthdays: Fantasy play at four.* Chicago, IL and London: University of Chicago Press.

Pence, A. and Nsamenang. B. (2008). A case for early childhood development in sub-Saharan Africa. *Working papers in Early Childhood Development*. Bernard van Leer Foundation.

Piaget, J. (1962). *Play, dreams and imitation in childhood*. London: Routledge & Kegan Paul.

Piaget, J. and Inhelder, B. (1956). *The Child's Conception of Space*. London: Routledge & Kegan Paul.

Prout, A. (2005). *The future of childhood: Towards the interdisciplinary study of children*. London and New York: RoutledgeFalmer.

Rakoczy, H., Warneken, F. and Tomasello, M. (2008). The sources of normativity: Young children's awareness of the normative structure of games. *Developmental Psychology*, *44*(3), 875–888.

Rogoff, B., Moser, C., Mistry, J., and Goncu, A. (1998). In M. Woodhead, D. Faulkner and K. Littleton (Eds), *The cultural worlds of early childhood*. London and New York: Routledge.

Schaffer, H. R. (1996). *Social development*. Oxford: Blackwell.

Smidt, S. (2005). *Observing, assessing and planning for children in the early years* (Nursery World/RoutledgeFalmer Essential Guides for Early Years Practitioners). London and New York: RoutledgeFalmer.

——(2011). *Introducing Bruner: A guide for practitioners and students in early years education*. London and New York: Routledge.

Snow, C. (1977). The development of conversation between mothers and babies. *Journal of Child Language*, *4*, 1–22.

Steiner, C. (1997). *Achieving emotional literacy*. New York: Avon Books.

Stiles, J. (2008). *The fundamentals of brain development: Integrating nature and nurture*. Cambridge, MA: Harvard University Press.

Tomasello, M. (1997). Joint attention as social cognition. In C. D. Moore and P. Dunham (Eds), *Joint attention: Its origins and role in development*. Hillsdale, NJ: Erlbaum.

Trevarthen, C. (1977). Descriptive analyses of infant communicative behaviour. In H. R. Schaffer (Ed.), *Studies in mother–infant interaction*. London: Academic Press.

——(1995). Mother and baby: Seeing artfully eye to eye. In R. Gregory, J. Harris, D. Rose and P. Heard (Eds), *The artful eye*. Oxford: Oxford University Press.

——(1998). The child's need to learn a culture. In M. Woodhead, D. Faulkner and K. Littleton (Eds), *Cultural worlds of early childhood*. London and New York: Routledge.

Twardosz, S. (2012). Effects of experience on the brain: The role of neuroscience in early development and education. *Early Education and Development*, *23*(1), 96–119.

UNESCO (1994). The Salamanca Statement and Framework for Action on Special Needs Education.

Vygotsky, L. (1939, first edition). *Thought and language*. Cambridge, MA: MIT Press.

——(1967). Play and its role in the mental development of the child. *Soviet Psychology*, *5*, 6–18.

——(1993). *The collected works of L. S. Vygotsky, Vol. 2: Fundamentals of defectology* (R. Rieber and A. Carton, Eds.). New York: Plenum (original work published 1982–1984).

——(1997). *The collected works of L. S. Vygotsky, Vol. 4: The history of the development of higher mental functions* (R. Rieber and A. Carton, Eds). New York: Plenum (original work published 1982–1984).

Wells, G. (1981). *Learning through interaction*. Cambridge: Cambridge University Press.

——(1986). *The meaning makers*. Oxford: Heinemann Educational.

Whitehead, M. (1990). *Language and literacy in the early years 0–7*. London: SAGE.

Williams, A. (2004). Playing school in multiethnic London. In E. Gregory, S. Long and D. Volk (Eds), *Many pathways to literacy: Young children learning with siblings, grandparents, peers and communities*. London and New York: RoutledgeFalmer.